PLEASE, I'D RATHER MANAGE MYSELF

MARSHA HAIGH AREND

Rollaway Bay Publications
Centennial, Colorado

Please, I'd Rather Manage Myself
by Marsha Haigh Arend

For further information, contact the author at:

Rollaway Bay Publications, Inc.
6334 South Racine Circle
Centennial, Colorado 80111-6404

(303) 799-8320
Email: mharend@rollawaybay.com
Web: www.rollawaybay.com

HB
615
.A74S
2003

Please, I'd Rather Manage Myself
Arend, Marsha Haigh
1. Author 2. Title 3. Business

Library of Congress Control Number 2003094562
ISBN 0-9743176-0-8

Printed in Canada

This book is dedicated to my father,

Richard N. Haigh

1921 ~ 1992

A perfect father,

A perfect friend,

A perfect mentor,

right to the end.

Acknowledgements

Writing a book is a collaborative effort. The first draft is easy, but the journey to transform a manuscript written from the heart into one that also appeals to the head is an arduous one. I would like to thank the following people who helped me with this transition.

Merrill Horine and Joan Haigh Horine were supportive throughout the project and shared their grammatical expertise as well. Robert Wood, Alison Wood and Kay Carpenter made many useful suggestions during the book's final stages.

Finding the right editor was difficult. As a strong personality, I sometimes find that people are reticent to give me their opinion. I knew JeanMarie Olivieri was the right person for the job when she wrote next to a manuscript paragraph, "Very funny! Cut it." Thank you for your honesty and superb editorial eye.

My twelve-year-old daughter, Katie Arend, brought perspective to the project as only a child can do. "You already said that Mom!" and other subtle comments helped bring this book to its final (and shorter) form.

Finally, I would like to thank my husband, Richard Arend, for his constant support and encouragement and for the many roles he played in preparing this manuscript. His persevering nature, coupled with his willingness to share his marketing and publicity expertise helped insure that this book would have a readership larger than our close circle of friends.

INTRODUCTION

Some of us are born with the entrepreneurial fire within us. We are consumed with doing our own thing and being our own boss. We chafe at being told what to do because deep in our hearts we know we can do better. We struggle while working for others because we realize we have the stuff that bosses are made of.

Unfortunately, as one of these people, I have learned that desire is only part of the equation. The other part involves the mechanics of getting there. Those who take the plunge and ultimately survive are not always the smart ones. Often they are merely the lucky ones.

This book was written for those who want to *create* their own luck. Many business books proclaim they are the way and the light. The problem is that they are written by the CEOs of companies with thousands of employees in offices spanning multiple continents. Their advice is useful if you need to decide whether your cash flow can still support the corporate jet. At the other end of the spectrum are books written by aspiring moms who want to turn their kitchen baking operation into one that sells to buyers outside the PTA.

Where are the books for the rest of us who have serious businesses, particularly those that are women owned and run? I know I certainly never had a desire to wear an apron professionally. And while my office does sport a panoramic view of the city, unfortunately it's only from the second floor.

When I started my business, I read my weight in self-help books looking for answers to the problems I faced daily. I needed to figure out what to do with problem employees, cranky banks, unreasonable customers, children who needed more attention from entrepreneurial mom, and find ways to preserve my sanity as I multitasked myself to death. I wanted real, useful answers that I could use *now* and I wanted to feel some comradeship and be able to commiserate with the person giving the advice. I wanted to feel he or she had been there, done that.

From my vantage point twenty years later, I look back and realize that I filled the resource gap by seeking out those who were older and wiser and soliciting their advice. I also tried to insulate my business from calamity by spending tremendous energy searching for the reasons I occasionally got knocked off my entrepreneurial feet so I wouldn't make the same mistakes again. While these methods worked, they were largely hit or miss solutions and very time consuming.

This book is an attempt to fill the resource void. Its purpose is to make learning how to dodge the bullets of business entertaining, not exasperating. With humor and heart, this book offers advice from every conceivable source. Irate customers, unmotivated employees, children, pets, spouses and even space aliens make appearances to teach lessons that successful business owners need to know. This is the handbook of business for those who really want to get their businesses going, not just talk about it.

This book is the gift I have to give to others who want to share in the exhilaration of being the boss, not just someone who answers to one. I hope you will find it helpful in constructing your own roadmap to independence.

TABLE OF CONTENTS

▌LIFE'S LESSONS

Sometimes the method is more important than the message. This chapter contains an advisory that sets the stage for learning the secrets of management and reminds us that the answers to our questions are often much closer than we think.

The attainment of wisdom need not be an illusive goal. A childhood memory emphasizes how a simple trip to the library can bring the wisdom and authority needed by every leader.

The thing we fear most is the unknown. This is why sharing bad news brings relief, not stress, to naturally speculative employees. A tale about a company brought back from the grave shows why truth may be the best corporate sedative around.

Don't shoot the messenger is one of the cardinal rules of business. A heart wrenching, real life example shows how ignoring this rule led to an unimaginable loss that changed the life of a family and the course of a business forever.

A comical account from childhood poignantly illustrates a basic tenet of business. When others in your organization are better suited to perform a task, it is sometimes hard not to wrench away control, simply because you are the boss.

For entrepreneurs, it always comes down to cash. Cash may not be the ultimate measure of success but it is the ultimate measure of survival. This story about a nightmare construction project exposes just how vulnerable even the healthiest of businesses can be.

Examples abound of people who see only what they want to see. The trick is to see situations accurately, regardless of how painful the vision may be. The accounts given illustrate why even talented, capable managers sometimes fail to see the obvious.

Ah, the power of the retreat! This chapter chronicles a painful lesson learned from believing that corporate getaways build business loyalty. Activities that do build bonds are outlined to make sure the money spent to build loyalty actually pays off.

Many an entrepreneurial company has been put to death by the over zealous visions of its founder. Vision is nice, but good ol' managerial pushing gets the job done. You can learn to slay even the most daunting project dragons, one baby step at a time.

Putting your finger in the dike is one way to stop a flood. A better way is to pick up your cell phone and call for repairs. The problems that come from refusing to fix things permanently are insidious and are easily illustrated by real life examples.

▌ A Look in the Mirror

Here is a lesson on how NOT to forge entrepreneurial handcuffs that will keep your business small forever. This unfortunate story relates how easily a business owner can be sucked into doing instead of directing and the serious consequences that result when this occurs.

Sometimes it's fun *and* smart to take a page out of nature's book. By pointing out the obvious parallels between horse and human societies, it becomes clear that humans would benefit from applying the management principals practiced by their equine neighbors.

Work smarter not harder, *always* applies to entrepreneurs. The existence of overtime in an organization always spells trouble and typically stems from a system failure on the part of management. Hang on to your ego while the real reasons behind overtime are explored and tips to overcome them are given.

A rural/ranch analogy makes light of the inherent differences between men and women when it comes to risk taking. Gender certainly influences risk perception. The challenge is to make better decisions by factoring in the gender related predispositions we all possess.

▌ WORDS OF WISDOM

▐ MANAGEMENT'S ULTIMATE CHALLENGE

▌ Management Magic

Learn to harness untapped creativity by motivating your employees. Effective ways to motivate are examined through practical examples and principles borrowed from Psychology 101.

Middle managers are a necessary evil in every company. Fortunately, it's easy to rid yourself of middle management politics and make your team productive. Just follow the steps outlined to shut down gossip and jump-start productivity!

Sometimes it's time to bring out the heavy artillery. The management technique described clearly falls within this category and should be the weapon of choice for blatant, repeat offenders. Examples show ways to apply this tricky technique safely and effectively.

Pride in personal accomplishment still exists, although occasionally it requires resurrection. This story of managerial insight offers a simple solution to the complex problem of accountability.

How do you effectively defend the realm? With an irrefutable paper trail, of course. The trick is to get your employees to create it for you. Fortunately, the electronic age brings with it, new weapons of battle. Seven rules are outlined to make creating a trail both painless and efficient.

Fatherly Advice

▌▌ Secret Weapons

▊ A STRESS-FREE LIFE ▊ IN A STRESS-FILLED WORLD

▌ SURVIVAL OF THE SMARTEST

Even the most prominent business leaders fail in course correction. This chapter encourages entrepreneurs to remain strong and make decisions using hard numbers that will protect the business, not placate the interests of outside parties.

▌ FRONT LINE DEFENSES

Vulnerability is a four-letter word in business. Typically, points of weakness are only discovered after the damage is done. A list of fifteen items, making up the Achilles' heel of business, supplies the ammunition needed for building proper defenses.

There is no mystique to solving business problems once you learn to apply the nine-step approach provided. Even your employees can be empowered to solve problems using this technique, freeing you from yet another entrepreneurial chain that binds.

After drawing an analogy between bankers and tree sloths, the benefits of finding a source of cash that does not involve a bank is touted as a necessity. How personal credit cards should be used in a business is explored after relating situations where credit cards clearly saved the day.

One of the inalienable truths of business is that banks will only help you when you can demonstrate you don't need help. Prudent entrepreneurs must therefore construct a safety net in the form of backup banking relationships. An analysis of banks guides us to the conclusion that baby banks are best.

▌ OPINIONS THAT COUNT

A Final Word

The author cannot take credit for all that is contained in this book. Much of it came vicariously, from years of fatherly advice. Fatherly words of wisdom that were recorded but never published are shared to show that the apple never falls far from the tree.

LIFE'S LESSONS

Chapter One

Management 101

Managerially speaking, we all aspire to be the perfect boss. Management is, after all, a high art form, ranking right up there with parallel parking.

I'm sure most of us have read our weight in "how to" management books, and felt the momentary euphoria that results from being armed with basic principles that have been advertised as management cure-alls. Well, the management principles may work, but only if you use them. After twenty-five years and counting, I am still a management trainee. I have however, honed my list of lofty managerial principles and have found that reviewing the list on a regular basis has its rewards. I am far more likely to be an effective manager when I make sure the list stays prominently posted in my conscious mind.

The trick, unfortunately, is to *keep* the list posted in our conscious minds. It is easy to spout the rules, but a list of rules is not memorable. Instead, it is a tedious reminder that rarely inspires us to change our behavior.

The chapters that follow were written specifically because lists are *not* memorable. What are memorable are experiences that affect us on an emotional level. Emotions, good or bad, are what move us to change.

Each chapter in this book breathes life into a management principle that is critical to the success of every entrepreneur. Some are memorable because the anecdote relating to the principle is funny or heartfelt. Other principles are memorable because the messages conveying them are filled with regret or unspoken gratitude.

When you finish reading this book, "the list" will no longer seem like a collection of sterile management principles. Instead, it will be a group of old friends whose management messages exist as part of your own emotional fabric, ready to be used for guiding both your business and your entrepreneurial life.

I know that for some, breaking with tradition can be quite painful. For those of you who would like to make the transition a bit more gradual, I offer the following list to add to your arsenal of management tools.

MANAGEMENT PRINCIPLES 101

1. Supply all employees with detailed and up to date job descriptions.

2. Make goals and objectives quantifiable whenever possible.

3. Specify completion dates for all job objectives.

4. Provide feedback on outstanding objectives before reaching the due date.

5. Recognize publicly the successful attainment of goals.

6. Include all employees, at least to some degree, in corporate goal setting.

7. Make sure personnel policies are up to date and distributed.

8. Adequately define jobs by documenting procedures over and above what is provided in each job description.

9. Establish a managerial structure that will solve supervisory and prioritization issues in your absence.

10. Do unto others as you would have them do unto you.

Keeping these principles in mind has helped me attack daily management tasks in positive ways when my inclination has been to put people in time out when they fail to play nicely or send them back to work without lunch for more dubious offenses.

We all need to improve our score as a manager. Well okay, perhaps a list now and then *is* a good thing. After all, even Santa has a list he always checks twice.

CHAPTER TWO

THE POWER OF KNOWLEDGE

When I was growing up, my cousin joined us for a vacation at our summer camp in New York State. Timmy, age twelve, had just read a book on snakes and bored us all ad nauseum with his critique of every reptile that slithered by. I complained to my father that I was not the least interested in snakes and couldn't believe how much trivia Timmy had accumulated about such a disgusting subject.

My father displayed no sympathy. Instead he applauded Timmy for reading a book cover to cover making him capable of spouting off immense amounts of uninteresting facts. Dad left me with this thought. "If you will simply read a single book on a subject, you will find that you now know more than ninety-nine percent of the people who hold themselves out as experts on that subject."

I thought that statement was a little brazen at the time, but experience has proven him correct. I try to read at least one how-to book a month. I find that with the arsenal of knowledge it provides, I can often call the bluff of alleged experts, not to mention employees who persist in telling me what can and cannot be done. Knowledge is truly the great equalizer.

Whenever I feel at a disadvantage in a negotiation or in an employer/employee relationship, I quietly go out and buy an appropriate book to help level the playing field.

6

Knowledge in some form is always at the root of real power. It breeds the confidence needed to tell others how to accomplish goals and leads to decisions that are based on logical principles, not merely opinions. When your authority is challenged, what better way to quell the challenge than to support your decision with facts. It keeps your decisions from appearing arbitrary and cultivates respect for your decisions within the organization.

As the ultimate decision maker in your business, you must rule by being persuasive, not dictatorial. How lucky we are that sometimes the knowledge gained from just one book gives us all the knowledge we need to persuade the most difficult of adversaries.

CHAPTER THREE

BAD NEWS IS FOR SHARING

At every company I ever worked for the upper management tried to keep bad news a secret. People who were fired were "on special assignment." The company was never in financial trouble, merely experiencing a financial downturn. The company did not lose business because of poor customer service; the company simply needed to redefine its marketing objectives. What unadulterated garbage.

At most businesses, executives waste time creating smoke screens and employees spend time trying to see through them. My tolerance for this type of nonsense has always been quite low. Hiding bad news does nothing to build employee loyalty, increase profits, or retain customers. It does not get new business or develop better products. It is a total waste of time.

I always liked the phrase, "No guts, no glory," because it sums up the credo of successful small business. Be brave. Tell everyone the way it really is. You can make far better use of your time than thinking of ways to wrap unpleasant facts into cute little packages of benign information. You are better off hitting employees between the eyes and then helping them accept and eventually improve upon a bad situation.

Dale Carnegie, a legendary business author, tells his readers to imagine the worst thing they can think of and then to tell their minds to accept that circumstance. Once acceptance has occurred, the mind quiets and can focus on improving upon this "worst case scenario." What's good enough for Dale is good enough for me.

I tell my employees the facts, and then, as their leader, I try to set an example by calmly accepting whatever circumstance is at hand. This allows calm to spread throughout the organization and focuses employees on building something positive out of the remains of whatever catastrophe occurred.

Here's what happens when you tell your employees bad news minus the sugar coating. Your employees:

1. respect you more because they appreciate being told the truth without packaging.

2. no longer expend energy trying to guess "the real story."

3. no longer waste time conjecturing about possible problems they believe you may be trying to hide.

4. bring their problem solving abilities to bear in order to improve the situation.

5. let you know how they view the situation as well as what action they expect to take.

6. take the situation seriously, work harder and socialize less.

The old adage that adversity pulls people together is as true today as it has been historically. People love to fight when they have a cause.

In 1984 I was put in charge of a nearly bankrupt and very demoralized telephone company. The first thing I did was to invite every employee into the conference room where I passed around a set of current financials. I started by teaching everyone how to read financials and patiently explained to secretaries, computer operators, customer service reps and engineers what could be done to control each type of business expense.

I explained that in my career I had never seen a set of financials as bad in a company that had not yet filed for bankruptcy. With everyone now on board, it was time to start the healing process. You could feel it in the air. Everyone had a mission. We all knew we were fighting for our jobs; no one wasted time on supposition. It was unnecessary.

Productivity went up like a rocket. Employees scolded each other for using Post Its® because they felt they were too expensive. We actually had a computer operator who figured out how to fix a printer with duct tape. The accountants used straight pins to make tiny holes in the magnetic check numbers of the checks to cause the automatic equipment at the bank to reject them so they would have to be processed manually. (This generally added two days to the clearing process.) The company was alive. The energy was awesome. Instead of feeling the need to be a cheerleader, I was swept along on the wave of "we can do it" optimism like everyone else.

The story has a happy ending. After eight months, we had cut expenses seventy-five percent and doubled the revenue. We made our first black dollar in that month, and amazingly, not one person quit during that eight-month period.

Honesty does work. People like to know how bad things are because seldom is the truth as scary as the reality conjured up by people's imaginations.

Respect your employees and deload yourself. Share bad news and rekindle the kind of can-do spirit that can make even a failing business, a success.

CHAPTER FOUR

DON'T SHOOT THE MESSENGER

Don was our operations manager. He did a little programming on the side and as jack-of-all-trades, kept much of the business humming along. He was very bright, but Don had a downside. He was easily distracted. His biggest distraction came from calls from home. No matter how busy he was or what he was doing, when Leslie his wife called, the world stopped turning and he would take the call. And what was the result? Don forgot to finish things. Don forgot to check things. Don dropped the ball.

One day a huge mistake was made. Invoices with a major error were sent out the door. This was an unforgivable sin. Don hung his head as he told me the news. And what did I do? I launched. I swore. I fumed like any good whiskey drinking, golf playing, good 'ol boy entrepreneur would do. Man, did it feel good. The primordial scream came up from my toes as I purged all the anger, which, for months, I had collected toward Don. I ended with an ultimatum. "This is unacceptable. You need to find a way to insure that this kind of stupid mistake never occurs again." He shut me down with one word. "Maybe," he said.

There was more meaning in that one word than there is in most novels. His word and his face told me, he had clearly had all he could

11

stand. He was tired of trying, tired of being abused, tired of failing. He had had enough.

Three weeks later Don resigned. I was not surprised because I knew instantly that I had blown it. For my three minutes of self-satisfying anger, I had chewed up and spit out someone, who on a good day, made a great contribution to the company. What I should have done was view the situation like any other problem that needed to be solved. I should have applied the problem solving techniques that had always served me well. Unfortunately, my entrepreneurial head had swelled so wide it no longer fit through the office door. I had partaken of the forbidden fruit in the entrepreneurial garden. I had satisfied my own emotional needs by blowing up and shooting the messenger.

One night about a month later, a story on the six o'clock news jolted me back to reality. Apparently Don, who had taken a demotion when he left us to work as a staff programmer at a big university, had been hit by a car. He had been riding his bicycle to work during rush hour when the accident occurred. He was killed instantly. He was thirty-four years old.

I shared the news with his ex-coworkers the next day. There was a great outpouring of emotion and of stories about Don. His wife, who called incessantly, had given him an ultimatum. "Get a job with fixed hours so you can be home to take care of the kids by 4:00 p.m. *every day*. Cook the meals, and of course, leave the car at home so I can use it during the day. After all, you have a bicycle...."

Don was mentally abused. Leslie was playing emotional chess with him, and he was slowly losing the game. Did I help? No. Did I even recognize the problem? No. I was too busy shooting the messenger to care.

If I had applied even the most basic of problem solving techniques, I would have discerned that his problems existed outside the work place. His co-workers were aware of his situation, and I could have gained this insight simply by asking a question. His performance was extremely erratic and did not track with the pressures of the business, which I have since noted, almost always indicates the presence of severe personal problems. I could'a, would'a, should'a—but I didn't. I was too busy being angry and feeling put out.

Many steps are required to successfully resolve problems. One step however, dwarfs all others in importance. It is the appreciative receipt of the message that tells of trouble, for we can only resolve what we know about. When someone respects you enough to tell you that there is a problem, don't blow it by retaliating. It is important to accept the message for what it is, merely the first step in the problem solving process.

I lost my opportunity to solve a problem, because I shot the messenger. The company lost and I lost. But worst of all, a strange twist of fate led to an unimaginable loss. We all move on, but I cannot help but wonder, would Don be alive today if I had spared the messenger that day?

CHAPTER FIVE

GOT A DOG?
DON'T BARK YOURSELF

Here is a bit of fatherly advice: Got a dog? Don't bark yourself. I have used this one at least three times a week for the last twenty years. How often do you embark on something that you are completely ill suited for, offer an opinion on something you know nothing about, or charge ahead to do something instead of letting the company expert do it?

Being a boss doesn't raise your IQ, give you more experience, or make your judgment any better. Big boss often means big ego, and it is appalling how many business owners charge ahead to do something that someone else in their organization is far better suited to handle.

We have all done it; we have wrestled control from someone who knew more than we did, and the consequences were unfortunately, predictable. This malady is not restricted to business owners. There are many examples in our own families.

I remember one early spring afternoon in Ohio when my dad and I went out to see my pony. It was still cold and the fields were sopping wet from the snow that had just melted. I decided it was too wet to ride and so, armed with my new red lunge line, I trotted Ricochet out of his pen and down the hill to give him a little exercise.

I did not respond when I saw him curl up his upper lip slightly and snort under his breath, as if to say, "Yeah, right. You actually think I'm dumb enough to run around you in little circles at the end of a rope? Let's see you make me." (Ricky was quite communicative in his own way.) Instead, I ignored his commentary and dragged his little behind (all 650 pounds of him) into a field used for riding. I clucked. I cracked my whip. I shouted, "Lunnnge!" He blinked his big brown eyes at me. "Yeah, right," he said.

My father was sitting on the edge of the fence taking all this in. As the "boss" of his daughter, he felt it was his inalienable right to butt in. "You're not doing it right," he said. The directions ensued. "Hold the lunge line tighter. You're not cracking the whip right. Hold it where he can see it." Now *I* curled up *my* upper lip slightly. "Yeah, right," I snorted under my breath. "I suppose you think you can do better."

He could no longer restrain himself. He hoisted himself up off the fence and came marching over, cigar clenched in his teeth, deftly hopping over meadow muffins as he walked. "Let your father show you how to do it," he said. His sole experience with horses had been two draft horses that he was once allowed to drive during haying season and a brief encounter with an obnoxious pony named Trixie that no one could ride until they were so tall their feet touched the ground. Well Dad knows best, at least that's how the speech goes. I handed him the lunge line and the whip. Ricky didn't stop grazing, he just rotated slightly, using his nose as his axis point, so he could keep an eye on this guy with the cigar.

Dad stood in the middle of the field. They made eye contact as Dad cracked the whip. Ricochet began a canter worthy of a Currier and Ives painting. Head up, neck arched, and knees high, he circled Dad on the end of the rope as if they had been lunging partners for years. He circled Dad twice. On his third pass, his head went down and his ears went back. Ricky drew his back legs under him, and with a powerful explosion of speed, took off in a straight line, a perfect tangent to the circle he had made, and headed at a full gallop for greener pastures.

Dad responded in a manner consistent with his *vast* knowledge of horses. He hung on to the rope. With one quick yank, Ricochet removed my father from his moccasins. Dad was frantically running behind the horse in his socks, making rapid squishing noises with every step. He still clenched his cigar. As he ran, Dad quickly evaluated the situation. The cigar fell out. The lunge line raced through his fingers and fluttered in the breeze behind a very tiny horse on the horizon, running in perfect form, a discernible smile on his lips.

Dad slowly turned around. (It's hard to walk with mud caked on your socks.) He meandered back to the fence in a criss cross pattern, looking for his moccasins, which he found imbedded in the mud, perfectly preserved.

He never said a word as he handed the whip back to me. We just had a quiet understanding that perhaps he had violated the "Got a dog, don't bark yourself," rule. Perhaps there were others in the family more suited to lunging ponies, and he should return to his perch on the fence where he could orchestrate from a distance, pride intact.

When I am tempted to wrench control from one of my employees, I often think of the "moccasin" story. Generally it causes me to pause, while I smile and then gladly delegate the task at hand.

When you can recall a time when someone wrenched something away from you, it is easier to resist the temptation to do it to someone else. Who knows? Remembering something from the past may even supply you with your chuckle for the day.

CHAPTER SIX

IT ALWAYS COMES DOWN TO CASH

Here is one of my favorite quotes. "Businesses don't go out of business because they run in the red, they go out of business because they run out of cash." The founder of MCI, Bill McGowan, is credited with this one.

I dredge up this quote at least once a month. Do employees think you print money in the basement? Maybe not, but it's Monopoly money at best and the object of the game is still to put a hotel on Boardwalk, where cost is no object. For most employees, the cost of running the hotel never comes to mind.

When a company runs out of cash, the game's over and everyone goes home. I make a point to connect everything we do or don't do in the business to the cash it will consume or generate. I try to dispel the Monopoly myth at every turn, for there is no other misconception as dangerous.

Particularly where cash is concerned, it is wise to follow the "half/twice" rule. If you want something to happen it will take twice as long as you expect; if you don't want it to happen, it will happen in half the time. Expanding on this theme produces the following corollaries. It will cost twice as much as you budgeted. It will be half as profitable as anticipated. It will be half as useful as you were led to believe.

In short, the simple way to prevent corporate death is to plan as if the worst is a given and then cautiously adjust your plan as the worst, on rare occasion, does not actually materialize.

We had perked along as a business for over ten years. During that time we had moved from our rented space of two thousand square feet, to a five thousand square foot building, which we purchased and refurbished in an older and more picturesque part of town.

In fact the local color was just that and was responsible for the shooting at the liquor store down the street. We also had entertainment provided locally, sometimes right outside our door.

One afternoon, an employee in a garden level office facing the street witnessed one of the area's fine residents breaking into her car and removing a package from the back seat. She came running into the hall, spewing the story at top volume. My husband (always willing to help) was committed to proving chivalry was not dead. He took his fifty-year-old, business-casual self out the door and ran down the street after the twenty-year-old, bag carrying, knife toting perpetrator. When we had collected our respective jaws off the floor, several (younger) male employees shot out the door in pursuit. When they caught up to Rick, he had cornered the guy in a dumpster and was calling the police on his cell phone. Yeah, Rick! Dumb Rick! Very, very lucky Rick!

So, when it came time to look for new space, we focused on a slightly quieter neighborhood, one where we *didn't* have fond memories. We just felt that the winos napping on the adjacent lawn did not add a lot to our client tours.

We selected the upscale "tech center" of our city. The image was right but the prices weren't. When a prospective landlord learned we were a computer company, we could see the wheels start turning. A costly build out would be our golden handcuffs. We would get a sweetheart deal on the initial lease term then, bam! The sky's the limit.

Well, we had done a reconstruction project on our lovely building in the original part of town and survived. Perhaps the ambiance was not quite what we had in mind, but the refurbished building had been wonderful. If we could rebuild one, why couldn't we build one from scratch?

No reason. We were entrepreneurs. We had experience. We smiled knowingly at the closing as we signed our life away for our building site that sported a view of the Rockies to the west. "By the way," said our real estate agent, "the building on the corner nearest you stayed empty for five years after it was built." "Why?" I asked. "Because the owners went bankrupt during construction. Fifteen-year-old company, but too many things went wrong. It just pulled them under." I hardly gave his comment a second thought. I would revisit that comment many times in the months to come as we navigated the seas of our own construction project.

We didn't want a big architectural firm. We wanted someone with whom we could relate and share ideas. We found Jim to be an affable and accommodating individual. I took some architectural classes at the local college that equipped me to complete basic drawings so I could efficiently relay thoughts of my dream office building. Jim turned these into the real thing, and we were feeling very good. Did I say good? We were euphoric, as we made sweeping decisions about flooring, brick and the latest in bathroom fixtures.

The months elapsed and we were finally ready to send our plans out for bid. Silence ensued. Finally I placed calls to all four of the builders. They all had the same answer. "We're sorry, but we can't bid these plans; there are just too many mistakes in them to allow us to come up with an accurate bid." "WHAT!" I thought. "You have *got* to be kidding." I didn't know what to do. I went to the community college that night and shared my plight with my professor. "Tell you what," he said. "Call Tom, he's a friend of mine and the principal of a pretty big architectural firm. Why don't you see if he can help you out?"

At 7:00 p.m. the next evening, I was sitting in Tom's office. He silently flipped page after page of blue print. "I know the guy who did these plans," he said. "He worked for me ten years ago, but I had to let him go. He made too many mistakes." I couldn't believe it. We had hired a legend. Well, Billy the Kid is a legend too, but I wouldn't want him as a buddy. How did we manage to bungle our evaluation process so completely? "Can you help me out?" I asked. "I think so," Tom answered. "But you're running out of time, we need to do a design/ build."

For the uninitiated, and that certainly included us, a design/build results in a turnkey building. The architect and builder work together to produce the finished product with the architect performing the management and due diligence functions for the owner. We felt the pressure lifting. Life was good once again.

At the completion of the drawings (which we of course, had to pay for twice) we had a small party and called our banker to give him the good news. "Send a copy of the plans to the appraiser," he said. "Will do," I answered, feeling smug about our smooth recovery from disaster. One week later the phone rang. It was the banker. "The plans don't appraise," he said. "Construction costs exceed appraised value by $300,000." "You have *got* to be kidding!" I said. "How is that possible?" "It's called gouging," he said. "The bank obviously can't finance these numbers." I hung up the phone, stunned. This couldn't really be happening. I was reliving an Apollo 13 space flight. I thought we had had our "glitch" for the mission. I felt my distaste for architects approaching my distaste for bankers.

I called the team to order. I stood at the head of the table while I *stared down* the assembled perpetrators. "The bank says the plans don't appraise. Obviously this is unacceptable. We are going to take our new plans and shop the bid in order to discover "reality." I looked out on a sea of little bad boys with their hands caught in the cookie jar. Mommy had caught them. Now they would have to play inside. They could not go out to rape and pillage the business community until after lunch.

When the bids came back, the highest number was still $250,000 under the original design/build number. We awarded the contract and a bedraggled expression of confidence tentatively returned to our faces as our attorney explained to the design/build boys that they were not going to be paid their "management" fees.

Construction, miraculously, started on schedule. On day eighteen of the nine-month project, we got a call from the construction foreman. We had failed to hit granite at the expected depth when excavating for the foundation. We would have to keep digging. We would be using $15,000 of the $60,000 contingency fund. While not happy, I knew that was why we had a reserve. With a sigh, we gave our permission to proceed.

The next week it rained. The phone ran again. The dug foundation had now flooded, and pumps would have to be brought in to drain it so work could continue. Eight thousand contingency dollars later, we said good-bye to both the water and the money. The dramatic stairway wasn't drawn with supports to hold it up. They would have to be added. The architects magnanimously offered to split the cost with us, and so it went, month after month.

By month two, we had breezed through the $60,000 contingency fund. By month four, we had put another $50,000 out of our own pocket into the project to keep it going. For the uninitiated, when you construct a building you literally sign your life away. The loan is considered unsecured because, as the banks say, they are financing a hole in the ground until construction is complete. For this reason, you must pledge every stinking asset you have during the construction phase, up to and including the dog.

We started to worry. While the business had some surplus cash, we were whipping through it at an alarming rate. At the time construction neared completion, we had spent an additional $210,000. We were nearly bankrupt ourselves. As we desperately awaited the closing date on our permanent financing, the dreaded phone rang once again. Our friendly banker was calling to tell us there was a mistake in the paper work. Apparently, a clerk had failed to accurately determine our required investment in the project and we were short $50,000. "When do we have to come up with that?" I asked. "I need it by two o'clock," he said without emotion. Fortunately, I was sitting down. "Come on, Joe," I said. "You've *got* to be kidding." "I'm quite serious," he said. (A requirement for being a banker is that you must be totally devoid of humor at all times.) "Fine," I said. "I'll call you back."

I went down to the bank with my credit cards. We were totally tapped out. This was it. I laid the cards on the counter, as the slightly surprised teller accommodated my request and deposited the advance in my account.

Well, we did make the payment. The final over run exceeded $250,000. It was only dumb luck that we had enough liquid assets to allow us to come up with enough cash to keep the project going without needing to sell the "untouchable" assets securing the construction loan. I have never been so scared in my life.

The building on the corner held new significance. I now knew how a perfectly sound business could be pulled under by a project that gained a life of its own. You can't stop, you can't go forward... you can only die a slow and agonizing death while being crushed to death by debt you are powerless to relieve.

We were lucky. We lived to fight another day, while the lesson, IT ALL COMES DOWN TO CASH, was indelibly etched in our brains. It gave me a new respect for the vulnerability of every business. Regardless of size, you are always just a step away from events that can drain even the deepest coffers.

For entrepreneurs, it always comes down to cash. Cash may not be the ultimate measure of success, but it is the ultimate measure of survival.

CHAPTER SEVEN

DELUSIONS ARE DEADLY

It is well known that entrepreneurs are capable of seeing only what they want to see despite a torrent of evidence to the contrary. Be it an emotional survival technique or merely wishful thinking, delusional thinking must be overcome, for the road that leads to OZ is maintained by the same crew that paves the way to bankruptcy.

I first met Jack when I began working as a consultant for the company he was managing. Jack had been a successful sales executive for twenty years. He was affable and could raise the enthusiasm of a group merely by entering the room. As the newly appointed CEO, Jack now had bottom line responsibility and, for the first time in his career, things were not going well. Being king of charisma was no longer the asset that could assure his success. The fear in Jack's demeanor was unmistakable.

Soon after I arrived, it became obvious that the company was in trouble. The first clue came from an IRS agent who came to attach a notice to the office door announcing that the IRS owned all the property within. Another clue came from the accounting manager who each week coupled her request to hold our paychecks with a heartfelt emotional appeal. Knowing that an emotional display by any accountant is a miraculous sign in itself, we all took her appeals very seriously and accepted the fact that the company must be on the brink of failure.

One day the directors of the company came to me and explained that things were not very rosy (no joke!) and asked me to replace Jack. I suppose my "mixed bag" of experience which included accounting and law made me an attractive candidate to the directors who were facing the loss of every personal asset they owned and were desperate to find a replacement for Mr. Charisma.

With great trepidation I accepted, feeling both afraid of what I might find and worried about how I might be found personally liable for the past sins of a debt-riddled company. My fears were well-founded. I discovered that the company was technically bankrupt, as the company's meager assets paled in comparison to its mountain of debt.

As I settled in behind my inherited eight-foot mahogany desk, which afforded a panoramic view of the Rocky Mountains, there was a knock at the door. In entered a well-dressed adult pulling a little red wagon full of plants. "At least I have a grown-up job," I thought smugly, as I shook his hand.

The man flashed a cheerful smile. "Your plants are here!" he said. "What plants?" I asked. The ones you rented last week!" he said brightly. "Aren't you J. Edwards?" "No, that was my predecessor," I said. "You're going to have to take the plants back. I've just taken over and the company is in no financial shape to rent plants or much of anything else. Just how much does it cost to rent plants anyway?" He dutifully stayed in his sales mode as he responded. "Now we come in and water twice a week, you never have to touch them. We prune out the dead leaves and if one dies we replace it just like that!" and he snapped his fingers as if the replacement was going to occur by magic. "Fine, how much?" I repeated. "Only $8,200.00 per year." "Thanks for stopping by," I said. "If things turn around sufficiently, I'll give you a call."

Historically, when Jack had encountered a problem in his sales organization, he countered by attempting to build morale to encourage productivity. To him renting plants truly made sense. They improved the environment and sent a signal to the troops that things were not really that bad. His response was certainly understandable but hardly appropriate. It might have been a great response if the problem had been morale and not a shortage of cash.

One of the reasons my predecessor failed to save the company was now glaringly apparent. Jack not only traveled the road to OZ, he lived there too.

When Jack became overwhelmed by circumstances he did not understand, he became fearful and lost his ability to objectively observe and appropriately respond. Consumed by fear, he turned to his past for answers and attempted to apply problem-solving techniques that had worked before, even when the technique was inappropriate for the problem at hand. Jack, in the face of confusion sought what was familiar. He had clearly taken up residence in the land of wishful thinking.

Anyone can be paralyzed by fear. The trick is to overcome the paralysis and to continue to make sound decisions despite emotional reactions. Always begin by rooting decisions in facts that pertain solely to the problem at hand. Try to observe, not judge; measure, not estimate; ask, not guess. After you have tried hard to prevent your fears from coloring your observations, try even harder to formulate a conclusion based on facts alone. If the conclusion you draw after analyzing the data really sets your teeth on edge, good for you! A decision that makes you feel uneasy is probably the right one because it obviously wasn't made with increasing your comfort in mind.

Finally, if you suspect a decision you are making is being colored by personal fears, run the decision by another person who is uninterested in the outcome. Sometimes outside perspective is all you need to neutralize your fears. It can also help you decide something very important. Do you make your decisions from your castle in OZ or from your residence in Kansas?

CHAPTER EIGHT

THE MYTH OF CORPORATE BONDING

Turnover is a problem for all businesses and our company was no exception. We had offered virtually all of the employment goodies that were in vogue at the time, yet it seemed to make very little difference in our turnover rate. After careful consideration, we decided to take the big plunge. We planned a two-day getaway for the entire company.

This was not as grandiose as it seems, as we only employed about fifteen people at the time, but after including spouses, children and significant others, our ranks swelled to over thirty.

We were looking forward to the bonding that every business article touted as the major benefit of corporate retreats. Would we abandon our senses and do away with corporate politics? Would employees no longer care who made the most money or had the largest number of reportees? Would everyone think twice before quitting because they would be leaving their network of friends, peers and the business owners who offered them employment?

We went to a rustic mountain retreat without TVs in the rooms. Despite the lack of creature comforts, our day was more than full, compliments of the hotel concierge who had tactfully suggested that our trail ride be cancelled and snowmobiling substituted after noting that a spring snowfall of over a foot had occurred overnight.

No one knew how to snowmobile, but we all warmed to the idea immediately. We broke up into groups of three or four and revved up our engines, while positioning our fannies on the electrically heated seats. With a wave of his mitten, our group leader was off, and our band of merry geeks forgot their business priorities in favor of dashing through the snow and dodging snowballs hurled by competing small groups. Everyone had a great time. Work was all but ignored and we all enjoyed being unencumbered by the worries of civilization.

After dinner, we returned everyone's focus briefly to the future of the business. We shared our vision for the future, explained our strategic direction and spoke with encouragement about the company's future. The retreat was hailed as a howling success by all in attendance and remained a topic of conversation for many weeks.

Unfortunately, a year later, less than half of the employees in attendance at the retreat remained with the company to reminisce about our weekend of corporate bonding.

Far from endearing them to the company, the only change I could detect was that after departing from the business, those employees who left maintained a regular e-mail correspondence with their former coworkers (during business hours, of course). It did nothing to build their loyalty to the organization. They were not grateful for an all expense paid vacation. On the contrary, the fact that we could afford such an outing convinced them that we would survive just fine should they wish to depart for apparently greener pastures.

Here is the lesson I learned. Retreats build bonds between individuals, not between employees and "the organization." If you want to build loyalty, you must build it between yourself and the people you employ. It's not much different from the established theory that captives can actually become sympathetic to their kidnappers if they get to know them on a personal level. The loyalty built needs to be to you, not to your company.

Aside from the ever famous golden handcuffs (which entrepreneurs cannot begin to afford), bonds between the company and an individual are tenuous at best. If they exist at all, they will come from an individual's sense of pride resulting from her belief that she has been directly responsible for the success and growth of the business. While this feeling can be nurtured, such nurturing is best accomplished in a business setting where personal accomplishments can be made a center stage attraction, not in the relaxed, casual environment of a retreat.

There are several ways to build bonds with your employees, and none of these involve a retreat. First, without becoming buddies, humanize yourself in your employee's eyes. Let them know that entrepreneurs are human too. Unobtrusively make them aware of the struggles you endure and the sacrifices you make to keep their world consistent and something they can depend on. Let them know that during an economic crunch you go without pay or that you willingly invest additional money in the company so that health care benefits do not have to be cut. Also make sure your employees understand that the stability you intentionally create in your business is not that common and does not exist in many companies.

Be aware that employees believe that sometime during the night a big money truck backs up to your office and dumps in the cash. Regardless of how poor or undercapitalized you may be, you will never dissuade them from this conviction. Don't even try. Rather, take the tack that money from the money truck is plowed back into the business, not into your pocket, and therefore benefits the company as a whole.

Next, make sure each employee feels needed, wanted, and understands that you feel that his contribution is unique and valuable to the company by telling him so both publicly and privately. This may ultimately be the strongest card you have to play in the game to retain employees. Appreciation goes a long way toward keeping someone loyal to you and consequently to your organization. A well appreciated employee will often stay in the face of more attractive financial packages and more prestigious positions offered by larger firms.

Finally, give them ownership in the decision making process. Do not decide things in a vacuum. Solicit your employee's opinions to encourage them to feel responsible for the destiny of the company. Over time, they will take pride in the company's progress and they will feel at least somewhat reluctant to leave the baby they helped create.

Our success in retaining employees has markedly improved since we abolished retreats and focused on building bridges to employees in personal ways. In our transient society, retaining employees is an illusive goal. There is no sense of permanency any more; all you can hope to do is to beat the average.

Take the money you would have spent on a retreat and spend it on a family vacation. Bonding may not work with your employees, but it *will* work with your kids and the benefits from bonding with your kids will last long after your business is forgotten.

CHAPTER NINE

BABY STEPS ARE BEST

In the heart of every entrepreneur is the home of the grandiose idea. That creative spark and the guts to do something about it launches most entrepreneurial careers in the first place.

It should be no surprise then, to find out that most business owners suffer from a common weakness: the inability to take baby steps.

Even today, I sometimes find myself afflicted by this disease. I simply cannot believe that I can't implement something that, as a visionary, I see so clearly. Why then, do I often find that my grandiose ideas simply stay ideas month after month, or worse, year after year?

Here is the simple answer. You can execute a task but not an idea. To accomplish a goal, you must identify the tasks required to reach it and then manage their execution. Hoping something will happen is, after all, just wishful thinking.

I first realized this when it became apparent we needed to create a sophisticated web application. We had tried to partner with several entities and each coupling proved more disastrous than the last. The last of our partners quoted us thirty days to complete the project. By the time we reached month eight, the phrase, "implementation time line" had become something that inspired chuckles among the staff.

In desperation, I called the president of our vendor and regaled him with our tale of woe. "In addition," I said, "the message you play to accompany your music on-hold guarantees a turn-up time of thirty days. What a joke!" "Well," he responded, back-pedaling for all he was worth, "I'm afraid that's not entirely accurate. It takes much longer to implement a complex application like yours. I guarantee that message will be removed today." The message proudly played the next day when I called and the next week *and* the next month. We gave up. They gave up. Our overextended partners had tried to be all things to all people and ultimately failed entirely. They quietly went out of business, music on-hold message still intact.

Unfortunately, we were still on the hook contractually to supply a web solution to our customers. Although I was an accomplished software designer, I could barely spell web. Java still made me think of coffee. How could I possibly lead the charge to develop an application on a platform I knew nothing about? The project was just too big and I had just witnessed a couple of businesses that allegedly were well-funded experts, fall squarely on their noses.

Heavily motivated by the fear of being sued for breach of contract, I decided to at least ramp on the subject of web design so I could evaluate the situation. I would like to pause here to mention that being willing and able to gain a "critical mass" of knowledge sufficient to weigh all options is a very important managerial skill. It is surprising how often an investment in self-education turns out to be the only practical way to get the knowledge needed to make a critical decision. All too often there is neither time nor resources available to get the information any other way.

I started by going down to my geeky computer bookstore and buying *The MBA's Guide to the Internet*. It is a wonderful book and it opened up the World Wide Web to me sufficiently to allow me to evaluate my company's strengths and weaknesses relative to web design.

I began to analyze what we needed to do to meet our existing contractual obligations and then considered how the company could build upon this base. There was only one way to do this. I swallowed hard to quell the panic over the task at hand. It was time to break the project into its components, delegate these throughout the company, and make a leap of faith that we could get the job done.

I focused my own energies on high-level design requirements. The coding of database interfaces and several other complex components, we contracted out to a freelance developer who had successfully completed projects for us in the past. Internally, we assigned designing web pages, setting up servers, getting security certificates and creating production scripting to specific individuals within the company. We met as a group once a week to evaluate our progress and clear log jams.

In ninety days we had our web site up and working. Why? Because we had identified all of the baby steps in a giant project, found someone (by hook or crook) to perform each one, and managed those people efficiently.

Lack of task identification and project leadership is so prevalent in business today, it's scary. Somebody has to be willing to keep things on track and doing so requires both identifying and managing the baby steps it takes to get a big project done. As an entrepreneur, seldom do you find yourself in command of a small business that has pockets deep enough to allow the successful outsourcing of these functions. And what is *really* scary is that regardless of cost, wholesale outsourcing seldom works anyway.

I learned a painful lesson through abdication. However, I am pleased to report that I got my second wind and now realistically evaluate my personal skill set, leading me to the conclusion that sometimes less entrepreneurial vision and more entrepreneurial persistence can get me where I want to go. It really comes down to managing myself well enough to make sure my "inherent visionary strengths" don't strangle the business when all that is needed is a good ol' managerial push.

You must learn to be a chameleon and metamorphose from the visionary you needed to be to get your business started, to the manager you now need to be to keep it going and growing. You need to change to fit the needs of the business, not the other way around. This is not an easy task, but as they say "Variety is the spice of life," and nothing could be truer for an entrepreneur.

CHAPTER TEN

FIX, DON'T TWEAK

My father loved elegant solutions, like those employed by Frank Lloyd Wright, who masterfully married form and function. In Dad's own field of chemical engineering, he applied the same philosophy and routinely came up with solutions to technical problems that were both simple and permanent.

I remember him telling me that his problem solving skills virtually guaranteed he would starve to death as a consultant. One time he actually tried consulting. He arrived at a glass factory where he was met by a bevy of senior executives who trooped behind him, a sea of white hard hats following in his wake as he walked along, examining their process. As he exited the factory floor, he turned to the president. "I would like you to take me out to lunch before I say anything more," he said. "At least I'll get lunch out of this deal before I solve your problem." They did and he did, and in a single afternoon he gave them a permanent solution to their problem and never visited the factory again.

Solving things permanently is not a desirable characteristic if you wish to maintain a long-term consulting arrangement, but it is desirable and often imperative if you're a business owner struggling to survive.

Continuing to mask uncorrected problems by constant adjustment or unnecessary human intervention is time consuming and dangerous.

By "tweaking" problems instead of fixing them permanently, you can slowly strangle your business while you continue to scratch your head over the cause.

This behavior is certainly not limited to engineering endeavors. All people seem to have a proclivity toward tweaking instead of fixing things once and for all.

For example, in my data processing company, each time we test a computer program without following a procedure or edit a file to correct a problem without altering the program that caused it, we are tweaking.

Tweaking is bad because:

1. It is difficult to replicate precisely.

2. It is easy to forget to perform a required tweak.

3. It requires a higher level of expertise to tweak a procedure than to merely run one.

4. It causes delays while someone identifies the need to tweak and actually does the tweaking.

5. It makes training far more difficult because new employees must learn to perform a myriad of odd fixes instead of a few standard procedures.

In short, tweaking costs your business a lot of money by raising both operational and training costs. It also forces you to replace revenue lost because customers become dissatisfied with products and services that frequently vary in quality.

I am frequently fond of saying to my employees, "I feel like a dentist. Why do I have to extract ideas for permanent solutions? Let's identify why we tweaked and figure out how to keep from doing so in the future."

When you realize your staff is tweaking, determine the root problem and demand a permanent fix. Next, assign the project to the proper individual (never assign to departments, nothing will get done) and come up with a due date.

As a final step, bring up the fact that the fix is not complete at every public meeting until sheer embarrassment drives the project to completion. And please don't forget; DON'T TWEAK YOURSELF, FIX IT!

A Look In The Mirror

CHAPTER ELEVEN

PLEASE,
I'D RATHER DO IT MYSELF

Please, I'd rather do it myself, is the credo of many entrepreneurs. After all, that is how many of us catapulted to success. Okay, maybe catapulted is a bit strong. Nonetheless, we all know that success by our own hands is a sweet thing. It brings with it a wonderful sense of satisfaction that is difficult to equal by any other means.

When I started my company, I was one of three employees. Never a shirker, I relished rolling up my sleeves and plunging in. Despite being the self-proclaimed "I'd rather do it myself" Queen, I still found the business required certain skill sets that were not in my personal repertoire. I had to admit it was time to search for outside expertise.

I hired Larry, a programmer, to maintain the software system we had purchased and also to write modifications requested by our burgeoning client list of two. Although Larry seemed nice enough, he had a little problem. He made mistakes. Most were not earth shattering but every so often, he would make one that belied his formal education and experience. He was also sick a lot. Frequently he would call in on Monday morning complaining of illness, which, knowing he was a young father, I attributed to lack of sleep.

One day as we processed telephone billing for one of our two clients, we found that the total amount billed was $30,000 less than expected. I called Larry into my office. I asked him what the problem was. He didn't know. He couldn't find it. I couldn't find it. Things were getting serious, for even a naive, stupid entrepreneur knows that losing one client when you only have two is not a good thing.

I stayed at the office all night, desperately trying to figure out what was wrong. Sometime after 2:00 a.m. it struck me. There were no dollars on any of the calls detailed on the bill. If the price of the call should have been $2.36 it showed as $0.36. We had lost the dollars! The next morning I confronted Larry with my findings. "How could you make such a blatant mistake?" I asked. "Didn't you test the code?" Larry remained silent. I looked into his eyes, his very bloodshot eyes, as if I was seeing them for the first time. Well, in a way I was.

I certainly wasn't going to win any awards for perception if Larry was the measure. He was drunk, certainly not for the first time, yet up to this point his blatant symptoms had gone unnoticed.

"Larry," I said, "Your services are no longer required. Take your plant and get out." I pointed to a large rubber plant in the corner of his office. Well, he got out, but as the owner, I certainly couldn't. I was drowning in a pool of my own construction and now I had to figure out how to get out myself. My total programming experience consisted of a single college class in Fortran, a programming language that was popular when wooly mammoths roamed the earth.

I did the only thing I knew to do. I drove to the local college bookstore, bought about a foot and a half of programming textbooks, and went home to read. Three days later, I found the problem in the code, fixed the program, and ultimately retained the client. I was a hero right? Wrong.

This early "success" set the stage for a career-long problem. It left me feeling that I could always pull out anything, if the need arose. This of course, justified my desire to keep my hand in up to the elbow in every aspect of the business, just in case we encountered "Larry revisited."

In the early years, this method worked fairly well as we proceeded down a technical path I felt comfortable learning. Insidious problems began to occur however. The workday got shorter. At home, vacations weren't even allowed as a topic of discussion. I had forged the proverbial entrepreneurial handcuffs beautifully.

So here is the moral of the story. Control, but don't do. Read the book to understand, but don't perform the function. Review the test results but let someone else do the testing. Learn the procedure but don't write it. It took me a long time to figure this out as I coded my way into oblivion.

The correct definition of "keeping your hand in" is the following. Gain an understanding of the process sufficient to call someone's bluff, make suggestions or ramp up in a reasonable amount of time if the need arises, but do so ONLY IF THE NEED TRULY ARISES.

Knowledge is power and power remains at the root of every truly successful entrepreneurial endeavor. The operative word here is knowledge, not action. A wonderful thing happens when you control and direct your business with knowledge alone. Employees don't expect you to get their work done for them or solve their problems. They look to you as a resource, not as a solution.

Extricate yourself from the "do it yourself" syndrome. Learn to let what you *don't* do insure your company's success.

Chapter Twelve

Be The Alpha Horse

In my youth, horseback riding meant being in 4H and learning to ride and care for my animal. Everything centered on the relationship between the two of us, and my childhood was made far more pleasant by Ricochet, my Hackney pony.

Back then I threw him in with whatever other animals were at the farm where we rented pasture. For several years he was in with a mare and her grown foal. They picked on him some, but he seemed to cope. Later he spent a couple of years sharing a field with forty cows. One winter he amused himself by running between the exits of a large barn in order to keep all forty cows out in the cold while he remained the barn's sole toasty occupant. (While amusing to us, the owners did require us to break him of this habit.)

Eventually, we kept him at a farm with twelve other horses, where King, a big black gelding passed his days by biting everything that wandered into his path. The abuse continued until one day Ricky was cornered. He wheeled around and planted both hind feet in King's chest, leaving discernible hoof prints. King seemed to mellow considerably after that and was further kept at bay by the lead mare's decision to make him keep his distance from the herd. Despite my lack of intervention, Ricky muddled along and life was good. In the society of horses, things just got worked out.

When I returned to owning a horse after a thirty year hiatus, I found one more simple thing had been turned into something complex. Horse psychology was now the equestrian subject of the day.

People now spent significant energy learning horse psychology and trying to determine the identity of the alpha horse, or leader of the herd. Monty Roberts, a famous horse trainer was making a gazillion dollars relating horse psychology to the problems of Fortune 500 companies. Clinics teaching how to relate to your horse abounded and horse owners were paying thousands to high priced trainer/consultants to help them relate to their animals.

ENOUGH! Can there be no escape from humanity's desire to muck up (not muck out, I couldn't resist this one) something as simple and pleasurable as owning a horse?

Let's get back to basics. In every herd (whether people or animals) there is a leader. In today's psychological parlance, it is the alpha horse. This horse, in the wild, disciplines unruly members and directs the activities of the group. The alpha horse makes decisions to protect the group from predators and ensures the group's well being.

The important thing to note about horse society is that there is no question about who the alpha horse is. The herd does not decide things by consensus. Nobody votes. The majority does not rule.

Take a page out of nature's book. You are the owner. You better be the alpha horse. Discipline needs to be swift and predictable. Your behavior needs to be consistent and dependable. You need to make decisions that will benefit the group, not the individual. You must quell challenges to your authority swiftly and conclusively.

This is what an alpha horse is not. The alpha horse does not coddle individuals, tolerate dissention within the herd, show favoritism of one member over another, fail to alert the herd to perceived danger, or treat herself preferentially.

Just sounds like basic, sound management principals to me. Isn't it amazing they do it all without talking?

CHAPTER THIRTEEN

OVERTIME IS A SYMPTOM, NOT A DISEASE

In the data processing industry, driving people into the ground with overtime is a way of life. When you consider that a sixty-hour work-week is commonplace for many programmers, is it really surprising these employees, on average, stay only eighteen months before changing employers?

And what does rapid turnover mean to a business owner? It means high training costs, poor customer service, disjointed and ineffective work groups and destruction of a healthy corporate culture. It doesn't take a rocket scientist to figure out that overtime is the enemy. The trick is to figure out how to stop it.

There are only two reasons for overtime. 1. There is more work to do than one person can perform in an eight-hour day. 2. The person doing the work is not adequately skilled or motivated to do the work assigned. That's it. There are no other reasons. Okay, I lied. There is one other reason, but we will get to that later. I'm on a roll now, so let's discuss reasons one and two.

When you note that overtime is burgeoning in your office, it's time to determine the culprit. Regardless of the underlying reason for overtime, *you* are always the culprit. If the employee is inadequately skilled or motivated, you are at fault. Inadequate skills mean you either didn't match the person to the job correctly or failed to supply training

44

when needed. Motivation, of course, is also your problem. It's your job to insure adequate reward and measurement systems are in place and operational. And if a job contains more work than can be performed by one person, guess what? You are the one who needs to shift load between workers, hire more people, or find ways to reduce workload by controlling growth.

Get a very big mirror out. Look yourself in the eye and determine which of the above problems has your name on it.

Now that I have spouted the rules, I will give you the one exception.

I once had a customer service manager who was always swamped. He was often still in the office at 7:00 p.m. after everyone else had gone home. He didn't have any more work to do than anyone else, yet everyone was able to leave routinely at 5:00 p.m. leaving poor Jonathan to slug it out alone. Knowing that overtime is always a management problem, I looked hard to discover what was wrong. His skill set was a good match for the job. He always had his head down and worked diligently. He cared about the company. I was at a loss.

One day I inadvertently overheard a vicious fight he was having on the phone with his wife. It finally dawned on me. He didn't want to go home because home was a very unpleasant place to be. That day I learned the one exception to the overtime rule.

When overtime raises its ugly head, take inventory. Are the skills of the employee and the requirements of the job properly matched? If yes, proceed to question two. Be objective. Is the workload for the job something that can be reasonably completed in an eight-hour day? If the answer is still yes, look hard at the individual. Does the employee have a skill set adequate to properly perform his job? Answering yes to this question leaves you with the last possible reason—motivation.

Don't make the mistake I did however, and limit your investigation to the office. Expand your scope a bit to include the not so obvious reasons that may exist at home. You may or may not be able to overcome these issues, but knowing the real reason for overtime is critical to finding a solution.

Take time to identify the cause of overtime. It's the way to insure employees are driven to make your business succeed, not driven to find a new employer.

CHAPTER FOURTEEN

BET THE COW,
NOT THE RANCH

Here is my advice for women entrepreneurs: Go for it! Here is my advice for men entrepreneurs: Don't go for it!

Risk taking is one area where I think the differences between men and women are really significant. The inherent tendency of women to evaluate every stinking aspect of every problem and zealously analyze everything to death typically keeps their businesses small. I remember reading a number of years ago that the number of women-run businesses had just exceeded those headed by men. Big deal. The problem is that the businesses women run stay solvent, but they don't grow. They are inherently not adequate risk takers. They stay solvent, stay in business and never hit the big times.

Oh, but men are a different breed. They will jump off the cliff with relish and when the business gambles they take pay off, they pay off big. The majority of these high-risk takers crash and burn however, and the businesses run by these individuals, more often than not, quietly sputter out of existence.

Our business advisor offered this advice to me not long ago. Bet the cow, not the ranch. Since a horse/rural motif runs through my life, I liked the analogy. It got me thinking. What risks constitute ranches while others constitute only cows? I decided mortgaging my personal

46

residence certainly qualified as a ranch. Gambling next month's pay-roll might easily be considered a cow. Would risking an amount equal to two month's payroll constitute a cow or perhaps a small herd? It was certainly going to take some fine-tuning.

Despite the difficulty in labeling, the concept was clear and given my personal inclinations, right on-point. I certainly never bet the ranch, but I was also guilty of never betting the cow, even a sickly one. After much soul searching I worked out a way to expand my risk taking limits.

To do this I had to realistically assess my risk taking profile based on the results I achieved. I decided I was probably a typical woman from a risk taking perspective. I always managed to meet the payroll. I never defaulted on a loan payment. But I also had lost count of how many marketing opportunities had passed me by because I was unwilling to increase the financial risk I was willing to take. Predictably, the growth of my business had been steady but small.

To overcome my inclinations, several years ago I vowed to occa-sionally push myself into that "uncomfortable" zone and stay there periodically if the benefits were potentially significant. This was not a huge move, and certainly not one that I was able to quantify easily, but I certainly knew a good marketing opportunity when I saw one and I was also very clear about "how uncomfortable" pursuing a particular avenue made me feel.

The results have been rewarding, and when I get really nervous I give a quick call to the family attorney to confirm that we have taken prudent steps to insure that personal assets have been protected from risk. I believe that I have increased my risk taking by about ten percent. This is certainly not a huge number, but surprisingly, the results have been dramatic. I believe this is because my entrepreneurial profile was probably moderately aggressive considering my gender, and a push now and then was all I needed.

Most businessmen I know would be well advised to stop and consider what will happen if their "sure fire plan" does not succeed. It sure beats performing a postmortem. Pausing before leaping may well make the real postmortem unnecessary and insure that these risk taking entrepreneurs live to fight another day.

Next time you are faced with a decision, regardless of your gender, run your gut decision up against your predispositions. After making a decision based on your first inclination, ask either "Why should I?" or "Why shouldn't I?" as required. Lean a little more toward the side that makes you feel uncomfortable, and once in a while, decide to stay there.

Chapter Fifteen

How Well Do You Hold Up The Ceiling?

It is lonely at the top. No one knows this better than the entrepreneur. You can't confide your fears to employees; you can't be their friends. Why? Because they depend on you to "hold up the ceiling." Employees look to you to make them feel safe. They expect you to be fearless and to create a structured world that gives them a well defined job, a guaranteed paycheck and a stable work schedule.

The responsibility for making them feel safe lies solely with you, the entrepreneur. No one holds your hand, gets you new business, or guarantees everyone's paycheck will clear. In short, a business owner has no umbrella of security; he or she is the umbrella.

Entrepreneurs, by accepting the risks and rewards of the outside world must also accept that employees, by choosing not to fight on the front lines, want an artificially stabilized environment. Make sure you give them what they bargained for.

This means you must be the cheerleader when there is very little to cheer about. With you the glass must always be half full. Panic, or even grave concern will send a shock wave through your organization that will certainly cause a mass exodus.

During dinner one night, my five-year-old daughter waited for a lull in the conversation. "I have something in my pocket," she said proudly, as she worked to extract a tightly clenched fist. "I know you

49

are worried Mommy, because the business needs money," she said. "I can help cause you can have my piggy bank money." With a somber expression she handed me two carefully folded dollars, a quarter, and a dime. I stared in silence as I realized I had failed. I had failed to hold up my daughter's ceiling and had breached the all important "mom" contract.

At home there had been many discussions about the financial problems of the business. We were so focused on protecting our employees from feeling their future was at risk, we totally ignored the little girl who sat quietly at the dinner table. She looked to Mommy and Daddy to keep her world safe and secure and we had let her down. "Katie," I said, "This money will make a very big difference. We can use it to buy furniture for the lobby. When you come to the office you can sit on the couch you helped pay for. I'm very proud of you for wanting to help the family."

My pride in my daughter did not obscure the lesson her act conveyed. Katie wanted to make her world secure again and she was willing to give up all her worldly money to do so. At bedtime that night, we had a heart-to-heart talk. "We're not short of money," I told her. "We have plenty to spend on food and to pay for our house and for clothes. We even have enough for *some* toys," I said smiling. "The business just needs extra money to make it grow but even if it doesn't grow, we will still be fine. We will still be together in our house and Mommy and Daddy will always take care of you—even when you're older and you don't want us to. We are going to be *very* hard to get rid of." We both laughed, knowing that this time the damage had been repaired.

Even if you are not comfortable with the rah rah aspect of leading a business, it is still important to recognize that the cheerleader aspect of management (or parenthood) is of paramount importance in order to maintain a stable workforce (or home life).

Without the proper emotional support it is impossible to nurture a business so it can grow and prosper. When the bank calls to say they are calling your credit line, you still smile to those who pass by and respond with, "Great, how are you?" knowing you have no idea how you are going to meet the next payroll. When your biggest customer cancels his contract or goes bankrupt, you still keep your interview with the new sales manager. In short, you charge ahead letting your strength and optimism bolster the company (and even yourself) even when you are personally scared to death and have no solutions in sight.

If you share your fears, doubts, or uncertainties about what to do in response to dire circumstances, you have failed to give your people their "security compensation." If you fail to make that payment, they will simply look for a job that can. As an entrepreneur, you do not get this type of compensation but you do get something a lot more valuable; freedom of choice, both for you personally and in situations that control the destiny of your business.

You also get great satisfaction from knowing that every success is truly yours because each one ultimately results from your decision making capability. With all that risk does come a very sweet reward.

So, next time you are tempted to share your fears or insecurities with your employees as you would with a friend, stop yourself and remember, if you want to be a successful entrepreneur, you must always hold up the ceiling. It's part of *your* job description.

CHAPTER SIXTEEN

PRODUCTIVITY—
THE ENGINE WITHIN US

It has long been said that productivity is dependent upon the tools people use, not on the people themselves. Rubbish.

People can do awesome things without any tools at all, *if* they are adequately driven to do so. A lack of tools is frequently used as an excuse for not working diligently. The expression of someone's belief that his tools are inadequate is called adult whining. It differs from children's whining because it is done in a lower key and typically does not involve pulling on apparel when the answer received is NO. Regardless of who is doing the whining, it is frequently just a complaint that is poorly stated.

A number of years ago when our business was briskly advancing from tiny to small and insignificant, we hired Ken as operations manager (the head guy out of two).

We immediately told Ken of our plan to convert to a new type of computer system. Ken was very familiar with the system we planned to migrate to, and we explained that we would do so when we had enough customers to justify the expense.

To handle our burgeoning list of clients (five at the time), we decided to hire someone to do quality control and help us track statistics about our production. We hired Sheila and gave her the title of operations administrator. We thought it was a pretty good title. Ken however, went berserk when he was introduced to her. He fumed and he snorted. He felt his empire was threatened. He was sure that hiring Sheila was part of a company plot to take his staff (of one) away from him. He actually walked out into the parking lot and pouted. I followed him out and we stood in the handicapped parking space arguing about what the operations administrator was hired to do.

At the unemployment hearing, he stated he quit because he didn't have the tools to do his job. He said he was promised a new computer and that we didn't buy him one. The hearing examiner worked hard to stifle a chuckle. I bit my lip because I was not sure giggling would be well received. "Did the computer you were provided fail to operate?" the hearing examiner asked, as he looked at his shoes. "No," responded Ken. "Were you asked to perform functions that were beyond the ability of the computer you were given?" "No," Ken said. "Very well, I find that you were supplied with the tools required to adequately perform your job and that as a consequence, your claim is without merit. Your claim for unemployment is denied."

Ken was not unhappy about tools; he was unhappy because a part of his job had been given to someone else.

When we hired an operations administrator we were commenting on Ken's ability to perform his functions. With only five customers, he felt the addition of another person to check the quality of what he did and to track his accomplishments failed to recognize his abilities in these areas. Bingo. He was right! We were not happy with his performance. It was our dissatisfaction with Ken that drove us to add a person that no rational employer could justify hiring.

Why did he fail to perform parts of his job? Because he was not motivated to do those parts. Every person needs to feel his or her accomplishments are continually recognized. They need to feel that they are evaluated using quantifiable measures that make clear to all concerned how effective they are in performing their job. Finally, they must believe their level of monetary compensation or other form of remuneration fairly compensates them for their efforts, whether the reward is in dollars or is expressed in less tangible ways such as granting additional autonomy in decision making.

As in this case, tools seldom have anything to do with an employee's inability to perform his job. It's almost always a case of inadequate motivation. Over the years I have spent way too much time mired down in a search for missing tools or some other mechanical problem, when the real culprit was an unmotivated employee.

If you believe this may be the case in your company, start by examining each of the three elements of motivation; measurable accomplishment, continual recognition and adequate reward, to determine if you can do something to awaken motivation.

Remember it is always easier to throw up your hands and say you have an employee who is performing poorly than to admit you may be an entrepreneur who is motivating poorly. Before you let an employee walk out the door or decide to boot him out, examine how well you have met his motivational needs. Well motivated, he may be the perfect person for the job.

CHAPTER SEVENTEEN

A CURE FOR ANGER— COUNT TO THREE DAYS

Just because you are the owner of the business, does not mean you can vent your frustrations at will. As an entrepreneur, you must obey a higher power than a boss. You must submit to your employees and customers to the degree necessary to retain both.

I was always much freer to express my opinions and vent my frustrations when I worked for someone else. One of the "perks" of being an employee is the ready availability of a scapegoat. The boss is always there to blame. As a business owner, you cannot meet your emotional needs by shifting the blame to someone else. If you quit, both your financial and emotional needs will become infinitely greater as you lose your business, perhaps your home and your livelihood for the foreseeable future.

As if this wasn't bad enough, you must submit to your clients as well. Even more than employees, they must be humored, coddled, endured, and nurtured even on their worst days. Being an entrepreneur just means you have dozens of bosses instead of one, and surprise, they are all temperamental.

So, how do you stay even-keeled enough to endure a bevy of bosses? I have found over the years that the only way to survive is to count to three days. If I become angry with an employee or with a client, I simply do not talk to them until I am able to do so calmly.

Please note that I do not necessarily wait for my anger to subside. I still enjoy thinking unkind thoughts and dreaming up appropriate animal analogies while speaking to them; I just keep these thoughts to myself.

I find it usually takes me three days to keep that edge out of my voice that says, "You jerk, I would fire you on the spot if I had even half a backup for your position!" After three days I can usually keep a believable smile plastered on my face sufficient to allow both me and the object of my wrath to work things out in a problem-solving manner.

I am very honest when someone asks me why I haven't sat down with him to discuss the issue of the day. Typically I say, "I have a policy never to discuss a problem when I am too angry to discuss it calmly. I am not calm enough to do that today. I may be calmer tomorrow but if necessary, I will continue to wait until my anger subsides sufficiently." This speech always makes me chuckle. It brings to mind the saying:

I can only please one person per day.

Today is not your day.

Tomorrow is not looking good either.

Making this speech has always proven to be a good strategic move. First, I invariably get a surprised look in response. If the employee or client is mad, I can almost see the wheels turn as he recognizes, usually for the first time, that he is not the only one who is mad or upset. It also keeps him off balance. He typically assumes that he is the one in the position of power (that's just human nature). Not knowing the extent or life expectancy of my anger keeps him off guard. Also, he knows that he must wait until I am ready to discuss the issue, with no idea of how long that may take. That keeps him stressed and generally takes the wind out of his sails (a very good thing).

Finally, it amazes me how often waiting a day or two makes the problem go away of its own accord. It is astonishing how a little time helps even the largest problems evaporate.

When I am ready to talk about the situation, I do it on my turf at a time convenient for me. I always try to operate from a position of strength and waiting three or more days further strengthens my position by giving me time to explore my options and discuss the issue fully prepared.

I have learned however, that no matter how irritated a client or employee may be over the delay in being contacted, it pales in comparison to his irritation when he senses my true feelings of disgust, anger or desire for retaliation when I debate the issue prematurely. As all of us with children know, you cannot take back what is said in the heat of anger. Business is just a practical extension of family life. Sometimes putting yourself or someone else in time-out is the best way to keep the peace in your corporate family.

The regrets I do have come only from those instances when I did not wait the three days I needed to cool down. Although three days may sound like a long time, I have had situations where I actually waited three weeks to become sufficiently calm and I do not regret the decision to wait.

Certainly waiting goes against the grain for most of us. I spent much of my career dealing with situations immediately, and often the outcome was very unsatisfactory. Since I have implemented the count to three days system, about ninety percent of conflicts I encounter result in a happy ending for both sides.

I think the reason many of us don't wait is because we have been taught that waiting is tantamount to procrastination. Procrastination is putting off something that should be done. In this case, you are putting off something that should be done only when the timing is right, a very important distinction.

If you are reticent about trying this method, do a quick analysis and determine your own percentage of success in conflict resolution. Once you know your success ratio, use the "count to three days" method for thirty days and compare. I feel confident you will find the added managerial control this method brings and the increased respect you receive from your subordinates will make it well worth the time you spend adding this technique to your arsenal of management tools.

CHAPTER EIGHTEEN

BECOME THE ROCK

No one is immune from financial setbacks. They happen to the brightest and most talented just as easily as they happen to those possessing lesser skills. Try as we might, we cannot protect ourselves or our families from calamity. We can only learn to weather the storm while we wait for the rain to stop.

I always believed the sun rose and set on Dad. He was the brightest and the best among men and routinely hopped over the puddles of life with ease. One day catastrophe struck. The company he worked for closed and for the first time in my life, I saw my father forced to react to a serious financial blow. He launched a massive job search. He utilized his free time to rebuild a house. He dramatically scaled down expenses. Lines of stress became obvious in his face. Despite his efforts, he was at an impasse. A depressed economy and advancing age had reduced his ability to overcome adversity. He remained unemployed for well over a year.

From my perspective as a teenager, I saw Dad's inability to find employment as a serious chink in his armor. I became disillusioned. How was this possible? He always had a solution to everything. It finally dawned on me that he put his pants on, one leg at a time, just like the rest of us. He was still Superman, but sometimes his costume chafed a bit and made takeoffs difficult.

While I was busy watching the master deal with disaster, I failed to notice there was another master at work. Mom did not leap into action by implementing a disaster recovery plan. She reacted in a different way. She became the rock.

Mom displayed the enviable talent of being able to live in the here and now. Instead of dwelling on the "what ifs" required for planning an escape, she concentrated on shoring up herself and everyone else engaged in battle. Instead of donating her time to charities, she accepted a paid position with one. She focused on what's for lunch. She kept our world orderly. She made sure the structure of everyday life that keeps us all sane, remained secure. She kept the momentum of the family going by forcing the continuation of routine. She did not dwell. Most of all she did not complain. Mom was a trooper.

She could have easily thrown her disappointment and frustration in my father's face. She didn't. He was doing everything he could think of to rectify the situation. I never heard her complain about their fate, not even once.

When someone is doing all they can, sometimes it is important to be the rock. You may not be able to offer a solution, but you can offer stability and let those who can do something about the problem operate from a well supported base.

Sometimes the problems your business faces can only be solved by a select few or perhaps a single individual in your organization. Despite an overwhelming desire to plunge in and help, there are times when your personal involvement will add nothing. What *will* add something is your nonjudgmental support of those attempting to solve the problem.

It took me a number of years to learn who the quiet source of strength in our family was. Unflappable Mom. Dependable Mom. Mom the rock.

Sometimes instead of leading the charge, it's important to let the problem solvers in your organization *recharge*. Be the rock in your company and let what you don't say and do, really make a difference.

WORDS OF WISDOM

CHAPTER NINETEEN

NINE OUT OF TEN THINGS NEVER HAPPEN

One morning I was in the locker room of my athletic club, when a woman I did not know struck up a conversation. The woman said, "You look a little stressed today." I answered that that was very believable, as I had "a million things" I was worried about. "Look," she said, "I'm a management consultant. I'm going to give you some advice that if you take to heart, will really reduce your stress. Did you know that studies show nine out of ten things we worry about never come to pass? So, take nine of the things you are worrying about right now and forget them."

My immediate reaction was, "Yeah, right," as I gave her the nod and smile etiquette required. Her comment stayed with me however, and over the next couple of weeks I jotted down what was worrying me every day. Eventually I went back to those lists and marked down the things that never came to pass. Unbelievable as this may seem, nine out of ten things never did happen. I have always found it hard to ignore cold hard facts. I am a numbers person, and I had numbers.

Thanks to that woman, I have made a concerted effort to discount my level of worry and I have to admit it has helped considerably. I also shared this story with my employees who concur that roughly one out of ten things actually deserves the worry we give it. Try it yourself. It's just one of those strange but true things that is exceptionally good for your mental health!

63

Chapter Twenty

Half The Time, Twice The Time

My father bestowed on me many pearls of wisdom, all of which I tried to remember and eventually incorporate into my own style of management. Amidst this barrage of fatherly advice are several "gems" that stick out as advice well worth sharing.

One of the best of these is as follows: If you don't want something to happen, it will take half the time you expect. If you do want it to happen, it will take twice as long. Truer words were never spoken.

Not long ago, I heard on the radio that a forum of successful business people was going to be available for a call-in show where the listening audience could solicit sage advice. They proudly touted that those available for questions had successful businesses because they had all been in business for at least three years. Three years? Are they KIDDING!!! Most companies I know have enough start-up capital to last that long. During the first three years, most businesses are just getting warmed up.

Here is a news flash. A business is not successful until it is making money. Being "on track" does not count. That's just a lot of smoke and mirror magic. As an accountant, I can guarantee that I can make the financials come out to whatever they need to be. What I can't do is print money and give investors a return on investment without actually having revenue in excess of expense. What a concept!

My father's sage advice should be applied to starting up a business if it is applied nowhere else. It will take twice as long as you think to get your business going, to break even, and to reach your sales objectives. It will take twice as much money as you think to launch your product, hire your staff, fund your development, and establish a healthy cash flow. Competitors will appear on the scene in half the time you expect. Investors will be seeking a return on investment in half the time you have allotted and will threaten to take an active role in the business in half the time predicted.

One of the reasons that "half the time, twice the time" is true is because people do not understand that their perception of time is colored by personal experience. Personal frames of reference are irrelevant and should never be applied to a business setting. Unfortunately, personal experiences are rarely ignored. People bring with them all the baggage they have accumulated over a lifetime and apply it to a new business whether it is appropriate or not. This is frequently where the trouble begins.

You leave your job making $40,000.00 or $140,000.00 (it doesn't really matter) and start a business where you raise 1.5 million in seed capital. Based on personal experience, this is a bottomless pit of money. It is more than, individually, you would ever expect to manage, yet there you are, suddenly thrust into a fiduciary role with a very big bank account.

More often than not, this sense of sudden wealth contributes to the Pollyanna attitude coloring your expectations. The belief is, we can surely hit break even, cash flow etc. before the money runs out. And how long is that? Twice as long as you think. Far from a bottomless pit, it is finite, and those advancing the money do not suffer from the same delusions you do. They are happy to hold your feet to the fire, because even though they may be sympathetic, they still own a controlling interest in your business.

There is a happy ending to this story however. The key is to adjust your estimates, not your perceptions. It is not necessary for you to understand why something takes half as long or twice as long. You need only to compensate for this slippage by adjusting your time line.

Every programmer that works for me has an "adjustment" factor. I apply this factor to every time estimate that individual submits. Some estimates get multiplied by two, others by four. (Some programmers are simply more optimistic than others.) I have never stopped to evaluate exactly why the difference in estimation skills exists. I only care that the time they ultimately spend is reasonable and therefore billable to the beneficiary.

I have adjusted estimates up and down, depending on the subject, for a number of years now. Not only do I credit this technique with the growth of my business, I credit it with its very survival. Had I not made those adjustments, things happening in half the time or twice the time would have killed us. This is one of those wonderful business rules where the reason is just "because." Don't do what most entrepreneurs do and analyze this one to death. Just accept it as one of the ultimate truths of life because Dad said so, and leave it at that. I did, but well... he is my dad, and didn't someone once say "Father knows best?"

CHAPTER TWENTY-ONE

DALE CARNEGIE; A REALLY SMART GUY

I am very big on how-to books. This natural inclination led me to read Dale Carnegie books early in my career. His books have positively influenced my career in staggering ways, and I have reread most of his books many times. My favorite is, *How to Enjoy Your Job and Your Life.*

These books contain the common sense observations of a Missouri man and the advice he gives is just as germane today as it was when it was written over fifty years ago. The basic premise of his books is, focus on the immediate situation and attack problems productively by separating the emotional side of the situation from the pragmatic side. I think his entire collection should be required entrepreneurial reading. Start with any of his books; it will be time well spent.

Chapter Twenty-Two

Rules For The Road— Do Not Drive Too Fast

When I was in law school my criminal law professor opened the first day of class with these remarks: "The reason we have criminal laws in our society is to make sure people understand what behavior is considered criminal. Say you are driving down the street and you see a sign that reads, DO NOT DRIVE TOO FAST. A cop pulls you over. You ask, "What's the matter, officer?" "You were driving too fast," he replies. "How do I know what's too fast?" you ask. "You don't," he answers and writes you a ticket. "You see," said the professor, "laws need to be adequately defined. I have, however, an easy standard you can apply to decide if something is criminal or not. I'm sure you will find it very helpful. If Roy Rogers wouldn't do it, then it's probably criminal. Now all we are going to do in this class is fine tune this theory."

Roy Rogers, America's western icon of televised justice, may certainly be helpful in determining the bad guys from the good guys, but unfortunately, there is no Roy Rogers of business. Employees cannot comply with the "laws" of your business if you fail to make them known.

Start by making your expectations clear. Break them down by category. Attendance five days a week, eight hours a day is an obvious requirement and is easy to convey. How about being an advocate for your customers within your organization? This one's not nearly so obvious and certainly the way American business treats its customers bears this out. The secret is to decide what behavior is criminal in your business and convey the "Roy Rogers Code" to help employees adhere to it.

Here is a portion of our company's Corporate Code:

1. All employees are considered equal. No one shall receive preferential treatment or get a special assigned parking space. Everyone is responsible for cleaning his own coffee cup and must wait his turn to be served at the potluck.

2. Every employee shall confess to or otherwise make known, any client-affecting problem immediately upon discovery so that proper action can be taken and damage control procedures can be immediately initiated.

3. All employees shall work a minimum of forty hours per week. If serious problems are encountered requiring additional hours, such work shall be performed without grumbling or whining. The job will be considered done when the work is done, not when 5:00 p.m. arrives.

4. Employees shall not remove property from the company or make possible the transfer of property to those not employed by the company without express permission to do so.

5. Employees shall not divulge financial or competitive information to those outside the company.

6. All employees are to act as advocates for customers within the company and make servicing the customer their first priority.

7. Employees are to acknowledge that their "customers" may be other departments or individuals within the company. By servicing them, they are fulfilling their commitment to act as advocates for the ultimate customer.

8. All employees are to consider themselves customer service

representatives. Employees must be willing to perform any task needed to support the customer, even if that task falls outside of those expressly mentioned in their job descriptions. This includes answering outside phone lines if they ring in excess of four times during the day or ring after normal business hours.

9. Anyone unable to appear for work, regardless of the reason, is to tell his or her immediate supervisor or leave them a voice mail message if they are not available. Relaying the message to receptionists or other employees is not acceptable and will result in loss of compensation for time not worked.

Most companies have a personnel manual of some sort that contains a lot of the laws pertaining to the company. Unfortunately, many times the subject matter is restricted to vacation time accrual, medical benefits, and dress code requirements. The real "meat" of the code however, should be the ethical standards by which you run your business. Does everyone need to dive for the phone if it rings incessantly, even if they are not the receptionist? I would answer emphatically, YES! To me, this is one of the major tenets of our Corporate Code.

It has been repeatedly proven that children do far better in an environment with clear boundaries, even if those boundaries are fairly conservative. I think we should take this thought one step further. All *people* do better when their boundaries are adequately defined and the consequences of their acts are clearly predictable.

It is certainly unreasonable to expect people to be clairvoyant about what you feel your corporate code should be. Lower your stress level and that of your employees by doing some real soul searching and commit your laws to paper. It costs nothing to do so, and the benefits are significant. You will be rewarded with happier employees and happier customers, both of which translate into a better bottom line for your business.

CHAPTER TWENTY-THREE

bcc — YOUR BEST MANAGEMENT TOOL

For years I pleaded with customer service employees to document their conversations with clients. I begged. I bribed. I threatened. I tried embarrassment. I tried setting a good example by recording my own conversations. Nothing worked. At best, they made a feeble attempt, no doubt to keep me off their backs. They clearly saw no reason to type notes that no one would ever see.

I shifted gears. I developed all sorts of ways to "use" the data in order to make them understand that documenting calls was important. I created reports on average call time, open items, closed items, hot topics, quotable requests, and productivity reports. I drove everyone crazy while I wasted countless trees to produce reports that were placed in the recycle bin after a suitable period of "mourning" had been observed.

I took a hard line. I put people on probation for not following the procedure. Sob stories proliferated. Employees were too overworked, forgot, "thought" they had entered the contacts, found the system too slow, had access problems with their computer, and complained they were the only ones doing it. I felt like the mom at the store who was being asked by her child for the 100th time to buy something. I got tired. I caved and gave up.

The penalty was, of course, that I didn't know what was going on. For that matter, neither did anyone else. Customer service representatives (CSRs) not only failed to communicate with me, they failed to communicate with each other. Often several people wound up working on the same request for the same customer.

Because of my lack of knowledge, I frequently got blind-sided by customers. They assumed, because their problem was earth shattering (aren't they all) that I was fully apprised of their situation and poised to leap into the void to solve their problem. Clearly I couldn't leap; in fact, I couldn't even crawl. I had no idea what the problem was. The only way I had of becoming informed was to proactively march into people's offices and address them with my famous introductory line, "What's going on?"

One day, having just been beaten up by a client for not knowing about his latest crisis, I called a meeting. "I am tired of being beaten up," I said. "I am also tired of walking around and trying to extract information from everyone. It's like pulling teeth and I'm sick of it. I want you all to start adding me to *every* e-mail you send as a bcc (blind carbon copy). This way the customer will be unaware that I am in the loop, and I will be able to defend myself without wearing out the rug with my 'what's going on' visits." Everyone grudgingly agreed to do this for one simple reason. I was a broken record about being ill informed, and they were desperate to find a way to shut me up.

Immediately things began to improve. I could not believe how much stuff I was missing out on! A torrent of information blazed across my screen. I was empowered! It was awesome!!! When a client called, I not only knew what was going on, I could pull up every nauseating detail from the e-mail exchanges between client and CSR without leaving my chair or even hanging up the phone. The clients were impressed. I was impressed. Productivity soared.

I decided it was time to share the benefits. I was certainly not the only one suffering from information starvation; the CSRs were struggling too. They often had to cover for other CSRs who were absent, and they knew little about the clients they did not normally support. Based upon the benefits I now received from blind carbon copies, I asked all CSRs to also copy each other on all client correspondence. Once this process was rolling, the Customer Service Department underwent a transformation. It finally started operating as a cohesive unit. The CSRs could now back each other up with impunity and play the role of expert when their only weapon was a fist full of shared e-mails.

Because everyone had set up a distribution list for e-mails anyway, the time spent keeping everyone informed was close to zero. With a negligible cost and an astronomical benefit attached to the procedure, I no longer had to preach. Well, Okay, once a mom, always a mom. Let's just say now I preached to the choir.

I would like to say that I came up with this by thinking long and hard about the problem. Instead, the idea was born out of desperation. Regardless of its roots, it is possibly one of the most profitable ideas ever instituted at our company. I wish I had thought of it sooner.

Please run with this one. It's one of best ideas I ever had. I would love it if others enjoyed their businesses more and made their customers happier because of this one little idea. "Even a blind hog finds an acorn once in a while," my dad used to say. Well, this is one big acorn. I hope you find it as helpful as I have.

Chapter Twenty-Four

When All Else Fails, Read The Directions

(A Woman's Perspective)

You, your husband, and your kids are driving along in the car. You turn to your husband and say, "I think we're lost." "I am not lost," he responds irritably. "This road comes out on Route 86 a little farther on." You know you are right when he turns off the radio. All men turn off the radio when they are lost. It helps them see better.

The gas gauge approaches E. Tactfully you mumble, "Let's stop up ahead for gas. We can ask for directions while we're there." "I *told* you we don't need to ask for directions. I am not lost!" The kids in the back seat know better than to talk. They know Dad will launch if they do because unlike the radio, they cannot be turned off to help him see better. A small voice from the backseat finally says, "Daddy, I have to go to the bathroom." Like a trout, Dad bites at this one. "We'll stop up ahead," he says as his manhood is restored. Now bathroom stops—that's something a man can do and still hold his head up high. You, of course, take the opportunity to buy a map and ask for directions while your husband pursues getting the rest room key from the attendant—pride intact.

Reticence about asking for help unfortunately affects more than just men. Although they may lead the charge on road trips, anyone with a healthy ego can be stricken by this disease. Before we ask for help or take the time to read the directions we first have to admit we do not have sufficient knowledge to perform the task. In business, there are many reasons why we fear this admission, which has consequences much more severe than having a tense afternoon in the car.

I have lost track of how many times I have asked a programmer, "Have you read the specifications for the project?" or, "Have you finished reading the manual for the software you are trying to use?" Invariably I get the same answer. "I skimmed the important parts." Pray tell, what are the important parts? I wonder. Since the project is not done and you are scratching your head while displaying the glassy eyed stare of someone who is truly confused, just how important were the parts you actually read?

I ask, suggest, cajole, insist, threaten, and plead to get people to read the directions. So why don't they? Because it requires too much work and they don't think they need to. They would rather flail their arms and wring their hands for weeks than devote an afternoon to reading a manual.

Anyone who refuses to read instructions that are clearly required to perform his or her job is clearly a wannabe, not a going-to-be. Those who can discipline themselves to do things that require an investment in time and concentration are the cream that will rise to the top of your organization. The rest will remain worker bees. They may make a contribution, but they will never leave the rank and file. They will never become corporate stars.

Self-discipline can be learned, but the skill will only be honed by those who are truly motivated to succeed. Applaud those who thirst for knowledge and display this desire by reading directions. If your husband agrees to ask for directions, immediately applaud his management of self and reward him by giving up backseat driving for the day. (You could agree to a longer term, but it is also important not to over-reward.)

Most of all, be a cheerleader for yourself. If you take the time to acknowledge your need to acquire information *before* you perform a task, pat yourself on the back for exhibiting the self-discipline this requires. Remember that to cultivate the stars in your organization you should lead by being a star yourself. Learning to shine brightly is not always hard to do. Sometimes it's as simple as reading the directions.

Management's Ultimate Challenge

CHAPTER TWENTY-FIVE

EMPLOYEES ARE GUESTS, ENJOY THE VISIT

Every time someone resigned from my company I used to feel forced to examine every minute detail to see what went wrong. How did I fail them? What could I have done better? Didn't they feel at home in our company? After all, didn't I consistently bite my tongue and forego commenting on their lack of commitment, unending chatter, and their time off taken at moments critical to the business? What then, caused them to resign?

Employees resign for a variety of reasons, but underlying each reason is one basic fact. It is not their business. They simply fail to feel the loyalty to the business that ownership engenders. As owners, we accept that quitting is not an option, both because of our never-say-die entrepreneurial nature and because it would be financial suicide. Employees don't carry this baggage. They are not forced to solve problems as entrepreneurs are. Instead they often solve them by walking away. So what should you do about employees that quit? That's easy. Learn to accept it.

Treat turnover as a constant in your business. I remember my father telling me that he used to budget $100 a year for speeding tickets. Driving over the speed limit was a constant in his life. Did he drive recklessly? No. He just drove over the speed limit often enough that getting a certain number of tickets annually was predictable.

Each year you will lose employees. Although it is reasonable to do a postmortem to discover business problems that may be causing inordinately high turnover, beating yourself up over an employee's departure is pointless. Just move on, plug any big holes you find, and make sure that procedures, not personalities, run your business.

One legitimate reason entrepreneurs cry over turnover is the high cost of retraining. If you do nothing to reduce this cost, you *should* cry over every resignation. If however, you have documented job functions, training becomes a vastly simplified task, and you can reap the rewards of running a business that is largely insulated from both the cost and disruption of lost employees.

Several years ago, our accounting manager resigned giving only one week's notice. I was highly irritated over the short notice period but leaped into action to see if she used procedures or personal knowledge to perform her job. It turned out that a mystique of personal knowledge shrouded her job functions, making it nearly impossible for anyone else to perform her job without personalized training.

To insure that her departure was not overly disruptive, I sat down with her and had her dictate instructions for every one of her primary functions. Why didn't I just ask her to document the steps herself? Because the result would have been poor. Anything she wrote down would have been a half-assed effort done by someone with a short-timer's attitude. She would have skipped over things that were obvious to her but not to a newcomer. The result would have been inadequate to train a replacement. By forcing her to dictate the steps she performed and then executing those steps with her present, it became readily apparent where the holes were, and I was able to fill in those gaps then and there.

At the end of the week, I possessed a "how to" book for her job. The following week I handed the book to her replacement who was up and running in less than three days. Not only that, but I now possessed a step by step procedure that I, or some other senior manager could use to perform critical functions in the accounting manager's absence.

I have found that there are two ways to get good procedures. The first is to ask the employee to document a particular function and then to have someone else try to perform that function without assistance, strictly from the notes. The second is the interview technique I used with the accounting manager. Just sit down with the employee and walk through the steps, taking notes as you go. If you are unfamiliar with the process, your notes will become a "cook book" for any novice to follow.

Employing people is *not* necessarily like raising children. You do not wring your hands and try to decide where you went wrong. Employees are mobile and move on for a variety of reasons. It is not necessary to soul search each time you receive a resignation letter. Simply determine whether something within your control was at fault.

Some valid reasons are:

1. Failure to review, raise or promote.

2. Inflamed employee relationships that you failed to defuse.

3. Employee boredom.

4. Lack of training and/or educational opportunities.

5. Noncompetitive wage structures or working conditions.

These types of problems are often surprisingly easy to identify and correct. Examining these issues on a routine basis is the best way to make your level of turnover manageable.

There are several things you can do to reduce stress caused by the departure of employees. First, enjoy the presence of those employees who are reasonably dedicated for the time they are there. Second, take steps to routinely document every job function. Third, minimize turnover by attending to those things that can extend the longevity of each employee's term. Finally, don't beat yourself up when the ride is over and someone moves on.

It is important to accept that turnover will happen despite your efforts to prevent it. Not only are resignations inevitable, but those who resign are not your family. They have no inherent loyalty. They do not buy you gifts for your birthday or come to visit you when you're sick. You needn't feel a sense of personal failure when they leave. Their level of risk and reward is substantially below yours and therefore, so is their commitment. Just don't expect them to act like owners and you won't be disappointed.

CHAPTER TWENTY-SIX

YOU CAN NEVER TAKE IT BACK

Once I had a programmer working for me who was an emotional mess. She could not bear to have anyone working in close proximity to her, and contact with people in general left her stressed and distraught. She resigned suddenly over conflicts with others and complaints of overwork.

I knew that her skills were exceptional and felt determined to convince her to stay. I knew that it was within my power to protect her from the outside world sufficiently to substantially improve her comfort zone. Despite all this, she rebelled when I made the suggestion that she stay and give me a chance to insulate her from people and situations she found offensive.

Half way through the conversation, she told me I didn't understand and that she really needed to resign. Irritated, I responded by saying it was clear to me that her personality anomalies were the direct result of personal trauma. "I don't know whether you witnessed an ax murder, were the victim of some sort of terrible abuse, or were abandoned as a child, all I know is that something pretty dramatic happened to you and left you a mess." She sat quietly for a moment. "Yes, you're right," was her reply and she got up and walked out the door.

I achieved nothing by making that comment except the empty satisfaction of being right. Success is hollow if the desired outcome is not achieved. If I had kept my mouth shut at that point, I am quite confident I could have convinced her to stay. I have often been successful in similar situations since, now that I am older and wiser and keep my mouth shut when the only benefit of a comment is personal ego gratification.

It's important to evaluate what you say before you say it. Neither kids, nor animals, employees nor spouses ever truly forget, even if they forgive. I apply a little litmus test to every comment I intend to make. Is the comment likely to produce the desired result or am I making the comment to derive some sort of emotional satisfaction? Emotional satisfaction covers a lot of ground. It includes everything that constitutes "look at me" behavior, e.g. I am smarter, prettier, wiser, more patient, a better parent, a better worker than you. If you really want someone to be impressed by you, convince them with actions; words don't work.

"You WILL respect me because I AM YOUR MOTHER!" What a stupid comment. Respect can't be commanded, it has to be earned. Just because you want something, doesn't make it so.

And how long does it take to think through the comment you are about to make? *Not long enough for anyone to notice.* They will simply think you are distracted and have a lot on your mind while you pause to consider the consequences of what you are about to say.

I did a lot of damage over the years as my mouth overran my brain, on many occasions. I like to think that I have finally added verbal discretion to my arsenal of management tools.

Once mastered, verbal discretion is a skill you can truly feel proud of and the results you achieve will speak louder than any words.

Chapter Twenty-Seven

Chatting — The Seventh Deadly Sin

Nothing irritates me more than rounding a corner to see a couple of employees chatting, totally unconcerned that I am paying for and witnessing their exchange. What riles me most is that they typically show no signs of remorse. In fact, they often make me wait so they may conclude their personal banter before pausing long enough to let me interrupt with, dare I say it—business.

In my youth, I would not have dared to let my boss see me chat, let alone force him to wait for me to conclude my chatting before inquiring how I could help him. Things have certainly changed and not for the better. In business, chatting has truly become the seventh deadly sin.

I do not have any pearls of wisdom regarding chatting, only this advisory. Chatting is a blatant manifestation of an employees' priority system. If someone is a chatter, she will stay a chatter. A chatter's personal life doesn't merely outweigh her concern for work, it dwarfs it, and every little gossipy exchange will substantiate this theory.

When you interview someone look for signs that they chat. Their inability to stick to a business subject without detours to personal subjects is one sure sign. Also, when checking references, always ask the reference if they would classify the candidate as a loner, somewhat of a loner, social, very social, or social to the point of being a problem. Because people only give references that will supply a favorable response, consider "very social" equivalent to being a problem.

Also ask whether the prospect liked to work alone or in groups and also whether that person was well liked. An answer like, "Everybody just loved Evelyn, she was so considerate and supportive," should raise major red flags. Interpret this as, "Evelyn was always involved in everyone else's lives. Work was only accomplished after personal conversations were concluded." The message here is a short one. Stay clear.

Obviously the best move is to not hire someone who chats in the first place. Once a chatter is in your organization however, you have to address the problem and either get her under control or get rid of her.

I find the most effective way to curb chatting is by embarrassment. "Julie, if you can't find anything to do, I can certainly find something for you." I use this when a serious repeat offender is not smart enough to shut up when I come upon a chat fest in progress. Know however, that this will only work to curb chatting when you are around. Chatting will overwhelm your organization every time you are out of sight. A partial solution is to be unpredictable in your appearances and to solicit help from lieutenants in your organization who also consider chatting a problem.

Stop by your chatter's office frequently. When she and a coworker are engrossed in chatting, do not leave. Stand there and glare, and make them feel uncomfortable. Challenge the chatter each time you see her with, "Did you complete assignment X? Are you ready to go over what you did?" and always give a chatter a firm deadline for her projects.

One thing most chatters have in common is their inability to manage time. This generally means that they must be micro-managed, first, to get them to be minimally productive and second, to reduce the time they devote to chatting overall. It is not a perfect solution, but micro-managing your chatters insures at least a minimal level of productivity.

Finally, and this is very important, set a good example yourself. Greetings should be limited to a couple of minutes. Long-winded stories should be forsaken altogether unless there is a lesson to be taught or you need to boost morale. Be cordial, but be brief. Do as I say, not as

I do, doesn't work any better with employees than it does with children.

Unfortunately, we must accept that many employees no longer consider work a number one priority. The secret is to compensate by setting your own standards of performance for your company. Employees may not like it, but they will ultimately accept it as a condition of employment.

If I suspect someone will be a big chatter, either from comments made during the interview or from references, I steer clear. I have never seen a big chatter become a great contributor. NEVER. The bible says you cannot serve two masters, both God and money. Similarly, you cannot make amusing yourself and earning a living, both number one priorities.

Don't be like the woman who thought she could reform the alcoholic after she married him. She can't and you can't. Don't waste your time.

CHAPTER TWENTY-EIGHT

MY WAY OR THE HIGHWAY

What makes a business efficient is typically its ability to execute tasks in the correct order. As leader of the pack, it is your job to set and convey the corporate priority list. It is your employee's job to complete tasks in the order you specify.

Occasionally, employees persist in doing the things they want to do instead of the things you ask them to do. When called on it, an employee frequently counters with, "I was just trying to show initiative." There is no difference between this and the little kid who tries to get away with doing what he wants by being cute. Initiative that violates the corporate priority list is not cute; it is counterproductive and needs to be stopped. Employees who fail to perform tasks in the correct order are taking decisions out of your hands and placing them in theirs. They are usurping control of your company.

For three years, I put up with a manager who blatantly ignored the corporate priority list and did whatever he pleased. Dan used his considerable skills in ego stroking to compliment me on my ability to wisely set our corporate course, yet he ignored the direction I set. My efforts to nudge him toward what I wanted him to do consistently failed. In fact, his refusal to follow the corporate priority list forced me to constantly ask him what he was working on. Despite my efforts to keep him on track, he kept busy doing things that made trivial contributions to the company, never stepping up to the plate to do the things that were appropriate given his senior ranking in the company. Dan did things; he just didn't do the right things.

All of my little tricks to cajole him into working on the proper things didn't work. I asked him to automate the client tracking system. He ran the postage machine. I asked him to come up with client retention plans. He chatted with clients but never acted as their advocate within the company. I finally gave up and fired him. Why? Because employees need to do the right things to move the business forward, not just the things they want or like to do.

This was a very hard lesson for me to learn. I regarded my inability to convince Dan to accept and follow the corporate priority list as a personal failure. I had to admit that although I was adept at spotting the idle hands syndrome, I often failed to notice individuals who steadfastly refused to march to the corporate drum.

When I fired Dan, everyone thought I was an ogre. They didn't "get" why I fired a hard worker. What I fired was a stupid worker. Dan was stupid not only because he failed to work on corporate priorities, but also because he displayed blatant insubordination by failing to respect the priorities set by his boss. The three other employees who resigned in sympathy the next day made it a very painful decision, but still the right one.

Watch out for idle people who need something to do. *Really* watch out for people who do only what they want to do. Both are hazardous to your business's health.

CHAPTER TWENTY-NINE

SIX MONTHS AND YOU'RE OUT

Jack was really smart. Looking back, that was the whole problem. To me there is something awe inspiring about intellect. I am attracted by it, sometimes even mesmerized by it, but when the honeymoon is over....

This is how the story started with Jack. His interests were broad. He was a lively participant in every conversation. He could really get enthused about any cerebral subject. He offered sage advice. He sat on his ass and did nothing.

We all liked Jack. Any time we questioned why he hadn't accomplished what was set before him, he plied us with plausible, in fact, brilliant excuses. We wound up consoling him over the immense roadblocks he seemed to encounter daily. To top it off, he had a daughter with severe retardation. Our collective heart went out to him as we imagined ourselves in his predicament. He milked it for all it was worth.

He never met his objectives because there were always circumstances beyond his control that were the "real culprits." "Jack, did you follow up on that hot sales prospect from last week?" I would ask. "No, the timing's just not right. There's a holiday coming up and I want to hit him at just the right moment." "Jack, did you get that proposal updated?" "Almost. There are a few details I want to add.

90

We really need the tone to be perfect," he would reply.

Those may have been the words I used, but these are the words I thought. "Gee Jack, did you do anything today aside from working on legal issues for your daughter's support, talking to your ex-wife, coordinating your son's extracurricular activities or surfing the net for your own enjoyment?"

This went on for, dare I say it, THREE YEARS! One day Jack and I met with my husband, to whom Jack reported. When asked if he had completed an assignment to rework a brochure, he responded with, "I had to put other priorities first, but I am definitely getting close to finishing it." That was it. My tolerance bucket had received its last drop. It was about to overflow.

On rare occasions when this occurs, an unusual thing happens. A torrent of words come pouring out, but honestly, I rarely remember what I said after the fact. I retain only a general memory of the ground covered. Apparently the thoughts travel from brain stem to mouth without ever stopping at my center for conscious thought. My husband was kind enough to give me a fairly detailed account of what was said, after the fact. What I said apparently went something like this.

"Jack, that excuse is unacceptable. I have been extremely patient with you while I have watched you do personal task after task to the exclusion of the work you are paid for. You certainly do have other priorities that take precedence, but we are paying you to cram in the work priorities amongst them. I have watched you surf the Internet incessantly, work on your daughter's legal problems, take time off day after day for meetings with your attorney and your ex-wife, and conduct a myriad of other personal tasks you felt were important. Either this job is a priority for you or it is not. We cannot run a business with someone who does not feel what they do for the company is a serious obligation. I have listened to excuses from you endlessly while the projects that are critical to the advancement of the company do not get done. I am not okay with this. Something needs to change."

My husband Rick said that when he saw that I was going to cut loose, he leaned back in his chair and slid his shoes off under his desk. He knew I was good for at least twenty minutes. He was right.

When I finally took a breath, Jack responded in true form. "I didn't have any idea you felt that way," he said. "I have had a lot of things come up that have interfered with getting certain projects done, but I do think the projects we have targeted for completion are important." "Fine," I said. "Then what we need to do is attach firm completion dates to your outstanding project list, and you need to do what it takes to get them done by those dates." He resigned before the first project came due. Big surprise.

On Marsha's Barometer of Stupidity, this one ranks right at the top. Was I unable to detect the problem? Of course not. I had fumed about his minimal contribution for not months, but years! Was I confused about how to hold his feet to the fire? No way. When I "cut loose" I told him his performance was inadequate, why it was inadequate and what we were going to do to insure it became adequate in the future.

So why didn't I move on him earlier? There was one big reason. In a nutshell, he had my number.

The first sin committed was that I didn't bother to require him to furnish evidence of his accomplishments. I did not ask him to specifically account for his time. I didn't jointly set due dates for projects. Instead, I accepted excuses without reason. The second sin I committed was failing to make him conduct personal business on personal time. Somehow we had created a set of rules for the company and a special set "just for Jack."

All of these errors were made for the same reason. I was intimidated by Jack. Subconsciously, I was afraid of a confrontation with someone whom I felt had intellectual capacity adequate to challenge my own. I did not feel I was operating from a position of strength. In reality, he was calling the shots, not me.

I could have neutralized his advantage had I done one simple thing. I should have followed the six months and you're out rule. In twenty-five years of management I have learned that if someone is not going to perform adequately, it is readily apparent after six months. It is irrelevant what job he or she holds. Six months is always long enough to make a determination. To make your decision conclusive, at the three month mark (after they have figured out where the coffee pot is) set measurable objectives and set down specific due dates. Someone like Jack, who is smart and adept at manipulation, can make all the subjective evaluations in the world worthless. A good manipulator can easily put the required spin on things to make you feel sorry for him when you should be putting him on probation instead.

By using certain time points and objective measurements, you cannot get "caught" by people who are master manipulators. It changes the multiple choice employment test into a true and false exam. If the test shows failure at the six-month point, it is far easier to appease your conscience and act in a manner consistent with the evidence.

My goal as an entrepreneur is to *never* let anyone manipulate me to that extent again. While we were dinking around with Jack, we missed countless business opportunities and failed to grow the business. In fact, we actually lost ground during the time he was employed, as new business (which he was supposed to be getting) failed to materialize to replace normal customer attrition.

This rule is a biggie. At three months, decide what to measure with your employee and establish completion dates. At six months, evaluate the results. If the employee fails dramatically, can him. If he fails in minor respects, put him on a program and re-evaluate in ninety days. The process is simple. The discipline it requires, now that's something that truly takes courage.

P.S. After Jack resigned from our company we discovered that Jack's employment lasted less than six months at each of his next three employers. I guess we were just slow learners. Apparently our competitors were already faithful followers of the six months and you're out rule.

CHAPTER THIRTY

WHAT HAPPENED TO THE DESK GOODIES?

During the summer of 1975, my summer of entrepreneurial enlightenment, I worked for my father in his new employment agency. The agency was a franchise. For those of you who have not had the pleasure of being involved with a franchise, let me introduce you. Franchise is spelled: Let me take seven percent of everything you get right off the top and let's see how long it takes you to die a slow, agonizing, financial death.

The business premise was bad. The franchise system was bad. What could be worse? The people who worked there. Did I actually say worked? Their average stay was less than two weeks. There was no time to run the business; we spent ninety percent of our time interviewing and weeding through fabricated resumes.

Our franchise advisor (who ultimately was convicted of fraud) told us to keep hiring until a few people stuck. How many is a few? Is a football team a few? How about all the players and their extended families? Perhaps that's not quite enough. Would all the players in the AFC West *and their families* qualify as a few?

"It all depends," our advisor answered. "Every case is different." No joke. So, what did we learn as we careened toward bankruptcy? We learned to watch the desk goodies.

When someone comes to a new place of employment, the first thing they do is to begin to nest. They make their habitat their own by bringing in pictures of the kids, their own coffee cup, a plant or two, a jar for their M&Ms etc. When they are really comfortable, they go for the larger items; floor plants, personal stereos, framed pictures and spare items of clothing.

When they go, they try to surreptitiously remove the nest. They often rearrange the desktop so the disappearances are not so obvious. Once the process starts however, I guarantee they and their nest will be gone in less than thirty days. In the employment agency, we took inventory of desktops the way most businesses track toilet paper and paper towels. It allowed us to do damage control, to make sure sales leads did not walk out the door and on occasion, to beat them to the punch when their continued presence was driving the morale of the remaining group into the ground.

A normal business mimics this behavior, only the pace is slower. When the desk goodies go, the employee has severed his emotional ties to the business. He may not depart quickly, but be assured that he is actively pursuing other employment and his days are numbered.

If desk goodies never appear, this also sends a message. The message is the employee is not emotionally invested in his place of employment. He may stay for years, but his decision to depart should never come as a surprise.

There is seldom a valid reason why you should be surprised by someone's departure. It is certainly a part of doing business and the signs are almost always blatant. Paying attention to these signs is also very worthwhile.

Having advance notice of someone's departure,

1. allows you to politic with other employees to make sure that they do not see the person who plans to leave as critical to the survival of the organization.

2. gives you time to transfer knowledge and even functions well in advance of your employee's actual departure date.

3. gives you time to plan the person's replacement.

4. allows you time to smoothly transition customers, vendors, and subordinates to others in the organization.

5. allows you to do damage control when the employee planning to leave is disgruntled.

6. makes it possible for you to pull the plug first if you determine a swift, abrupt departure would be better for the business.

I'm proud to say that out of the worst business experience of my (and my father's) career, at least one pearl of wisdom survived. It's the little things that count. Make it an even more valuable pearl. Pass it on to an entrepreneurial friend who is currently experiencing the joys of personnel.

CHAPTER THIRTY-ONE

WHO PARKS BY
THE FRONT DOOR?

Not all business lessons come from inside the office. Some lessons come straight from the parking lot.

When we first constructed our office building, most people parked by the front door. It meant a shorter walk in the morning, and so convenience prevailed (at least temporarily). It soon became apparent to everyone that "Mom" (that's me, of course) had a bird's eye view of arrivals and departures, compliments of my second floor vantage point. I'm sure everyone felt I had nothing better to do than track employee vehicle activity in an Excel spread sheet.

Slowly a shift began to occur. The cars slowly disappeared, as parking on the other side of the building came into vogue. A few stayed where they were, and I noted that those who were both secure in their positions and punctual were the only ones brave enough to park in the front after the ninety day migration period.

The parking lot migration theory simply reinforces one of the basic truisms of owning a business. You, as the owner, will never be part of the group. You are the Mom, Big Brother, or sometimes even the enemy. Do not take it personally; it just goes with the territory.

Your role is parental in many ways. You routinely need to cultivate and criticize, encourage and reprimand and competitively evaluate and compensate those people who work for you. The employer/employee relationship is a contractual one that can only be managed at arms length. Attempting to establish a reciprocal friendship with all its attendant dependencies thwarts the relationship you must have as employer and employee to effectively operate your business.

It is not necessary to be friends with people who work for you. It just puts strains upon the work relationship that should not be there and ultimately one of the relationships must be sacrificed in order to preserve the other.

If, at times, you are tempted to strike up a close personal friendship with one of your employees, go check out the parking lot. Would a friend be concerned if you saw where they parked?

You are the boss. Control over the type of relationships formed is in your hands. Do not undermine the foundation of your business by destroying the relationships upon which it is built. Your friends should support you; your employees should support the business. You will all be happier in the long run if you respect the difference.

CHAPTER THIRTY-TWO

SICK DAYS ARE FOR WIMPS

When I worked for someone else, I was rarely out sick. The operative word here is "out." Sickness was something I just took in stride. I took pride in being able to ignore a fever or a little nausea. It never occurred to me to take three or four days off so I could take good care of myself, eat Jell-O and watch soap operas. I had things to do, people to see, obligations to meet. I was paid to work and so off to work I went.

This does not mean I ignored serious illness. If I was sick enough to require medical treatment or felt my presence in the office would infect others, I stayed home. I just didn't think feeling "a bit under the weather" granted me the right to burden others with my workload while I napped at home.

When I became an entrepreneur I had a rude awakening. I soon discovered others did not feel this same sense of responsibility that caused me to overlook my infirmities and keep churning out the work. Certainly the people I employed took a different view. They considered sick time an inalienable right and found ways to take unused time before the end of the year, for it would be a calamity to let perfectly good sick leave go to waste.

I really believe this view of sick time is much more a manifestation of work ethic than of differences in employer/employee views. In fact, were it not such a serious subject, I could get real enjoyment from recalling some of the wonderful excuses I have heard over the years. My favorite comes from Steve, a customer service representative who said he could not come in to work because he had fallen out of a hot air balloon and was in the hospital emergency room. Doesn't everyone hot air balloon on a Monday morning before they go to work? Too bad he didn't fall on his head, there was obviously not much in there that could be damaged.

Everyone gets sick. Some get sick and wimp out. Some get sick and stick it out. I have found it interesting to add this question to those asked of references supplied by job applicants, "Do you recall if the applicant missed more than fifteen days of work per year due to illness? Do you recall more than ten days? Do you recall more than five days?" Start high so that the reference thinks you are okay with a fairly high number of days out. If you convince them on this point, you will get a response like "Jim only missed a week and a half last year," or better yet, "Jim was a trooper, that guy was never out sick!"

I had a receptionist once who kept missing time from work. It wasn't always a full day. Frequently it was merely a two hour late start, a three hour lunch for a doctor's appointment, or the "I'm not feeling great so I'm going home early," reduced day.

She, of course, exhausted her sick leave early in the year. It therefore came as no surprise when she discovered her pay was about to be docked and asked if she could make up the time.

My answer was instantaneous. "No. Not only no, but hell, no." I took the opportunity to drill the point home. "In a small business, the issue is coverage, not hours. If you fail to appear or leave early and your absence is unexpected, the work does not go away. Someone has to cover for you. This means they must shoulder your work as well as their own because clients pay the light bill and cannot be put on hold just because you don't feel well. We are all tolerant of unexpected illness. However, tolerance is a matter of degree. Your absences are excessive and will no longer be tolerated. Any future absences will bring the response you expect. Your pay will simply be reduced by the hours you miss.

This speech of course, was designed to force her hand. Either she would toe the line or quit. (You always want people to quit; this is how you avoid unemployment.) Anne didn't waste any time. She resigned within the week.

Excessive time off for illness is an insidious disease. It frustrates both clients and coworkers. It destroys the momentum of the business. It torpedoes productivity. It causes a breakdown in communication among departments that can severely injure your business.

Don't be a bleeding heart when it comes to time off. If someone just can't seem to manage his life or his health sufficiently to maintain a consistent presence, cut him loose or better yet, cause him to conclude that quitting is his best alternative. Make sure that what you run is a business, not an entitlement program.

Chapter Thirty-Three

Who Pays The Light Bill?

Much to my amazement, most employees feel that money to run a business falls from the sky. It is the rare employee who really appreciates the customers who make it possible for the business to meet the payroll, cover the rent, and pay the light bill.

As customers, we have all experienced the symptoms of a business that is not client focused. Their representatives respond to your inquiry when it is convenient for them. They don't tell you they appreciate your decision to use their services or expertise; they are rarely sensitive to your problems or concerns.

Employees of these companies don't care because they don't see how improving their response to you will benefit *them*. They will still get paid without you. Their company will still furnish them health care and retirement benefits even if they treat you like dirt. In short, as long as they treat you civilly enough to retain their jobs, they have no incentive to go the extra inch, yet alone the extra mile.

The two biggest assets your business has are your employees and your customers. The success of your business is dependent upon whether your employees understand that the customers, not the owners of the business make paying the light bill and meeting every other obligation of the business, possible.

Your goal as an entrepreneur is to "put the fodder down where the calves can reach it," as my dad used to say. The consequences associated with the presence or absence of customers must be felt by all of your employees. They must understand the connection between their paycheck and the happiness of the customers they serve.

Without customers, employees don't get paid, yet managers often mask this connection in order to "protect" their employees. This connection doesn't need to be masked; it needs to be emphasized, for serving the customer is the lifeblood of every business.

Here are a couple of ways to make it clear to employees that their primary goal is to support the customers that pay their salary.

Relate the amount of revenue a client brings in to an average salary. "Sam, that delay in shipping really upset Milly at Modern Widgets, Inc. Their contract is up for renewal in six months. If we fail to renew them we will be searching for a replacement revenue source capable of supporting seven full-time people. What do you suggest we do to make sure we don't place seven people's jobs in jeopardy?" This may sound a bit cruel, but in fact, our goal is to raise the pucker factor. You want your staff to feel a little less comfy, a little less secure. They need to start seeing the connection between what they do and what the company can financially support.

If Modern Widgets, Inc. does not renew, conduct a postmortem. It's always important to understand why business is lost anyway, and through this process, you can reveal the gyrations you will have to perform to reduce costs and replace revenue.

When customer support fails and results in lost business, do not insulate employees from the event. Instead, use the setback to communicate that lost business translates into cutbacks or other adverse changes that affect everyone's work environment. The impact does not need to be big. Restructured bonus plans, reduced stock option or matching fund plans, or reductions in other perks all send this message clearly. Making the approval procedure for expenditures more rigorous can also serve as an effective reminder of the cause and effect relationship between what a business spends and what it has to spend. Adjustments should be gentle, however. The point is to raise individual awareness, not to arbitrarily reduce compensation to fix financial ills.

These are by no means the only ways to forge an appreciative link between your employees and your customers, but having used the above methods successfully, I can guarantee they will all do a lot to improve employees' understanding of who really does pay the light bill.

CHAPTER THIRTY-FOUR

GUILTY UNTIL PROVEN INNOCENT

Contrary to the American legal system, assuming guilt in business is generally much safer and more accurate than presuming innocence. I have never been blind sided because I assumed that things were bad or that someone was failing to do his job. On the other hand, I have been caught many times by assuming everything was okay, only to find out at the eleventh hour that nothing was okay.

People's pride is generally at the root of all problems. Employees don't want to admit that they forgot to do something, that they were goofing off and didn't get something finished, or that a client came unglued because they didn't make a commitment date.

The good news is that there is an easy method to keep unpleasant surprises to a minimum. It is called assumption of guilt.

"Mary, I think we may be missing a deadline for Wacky Wafers, Inc. If we do, we both know their manager, Paula, will go ballistic. Tell me what's going on. We can defuse if we need to, but after that, let's sit down and get a grip on where you are with commitments. If we need to get tighter on dates, we can come up with a plan. Since it's one of your performance objectives, I know getting a handle on these commitment dates is important to both of us."

Here I assume that the problem exists. I don't let Mary off the hook fully, but I open the door for her to tell me the truth about the situation. I do this by making clear that I accept the fact that there may already be a problem and that I am going to attack it with her by maintaining a problem solving attitude, which I also want her to adopt.

In the unlikely event that no problem exists because Mary is on top of things and the deadline is not in jeopardy, Mary is in an enviable position. Mary gets to respond with, "I know it's an objective and everything is on schedule. Paula e-mailed me to say how pleased she is." Now I get the pleasant task of applauding Mary's achievement and complementing her on her progress. It makes for a very nice day for both of us.

Now, let's assume I do not follow the assumption of guilt method. Instead I take the other stance, and say, "Mary, you know deadlines are critical to Paula. I assume you are on top of the situation and things are on schedule as expected. Where are we on this project?" Now, if things are not going well, I am in trouble. Mary's pride is at stake. If she tells me the real story, it's equivalent to her saying, "I failed. I screwed up again. Okay, go ahead and yell at me." To save pride, Mary will either lie (worst case) or dance around the issue, alluding to a "possible" problem (slightly better case), which will lead to confrontation, denial, exposure, justification and ultimately rebellion.

So what should you assume? Always assume the worst. Assume that the client is unhappy. What's the worst that can happen? You find out you were wrong and go on to something else. If you are right, you have intervened (maybe just in time), by digging in and ferreting out issues that may not have been apparent but are critical to the retention of your customer. Even internally you should assume the worst. Assume the accountant is pilfering money. It doesn't hurt to perform some checks and balances, and if nothing else, it will give you peace of mind.

The biggest reward from using the assumption of guilt approach is that once employees realize how this method operates, they will bring problems to you without your solicitation. They will do this because they will learn you are willing to help them solve problems without recrimination. This is truly a milestone, for once this occurs, your clairvoyant talents will be less critical to the success of your business.

The object of the game is for employees to come to you. This will happen consistently if you do two things. First, follow the assumption of guilt management principle. Second, respond consistently to like situations. Not only must you respond appropriately, you must respond the same way *every time.* There cannot be exceptions for bad moods, PMS, the dog died, some client yelled at me today, etc.

If I could make a business wish, I would wish never to have to say to another client, "Gee, I am not aware of the situation, but let me check into it and get right back to you." Wouldn't it be nice to always be able to say, "Yes, I am aware of the situation, and here are the details of what we are doing about it."

There are good reasons why you should never confuse the legal principle of presumption of innocence with the management principle of presumption of guilt. The evidence speaks for itself.

CHAPTER THIRTY-FIVE

CALL IN, CALL OFTEN, CALL UNPREDICTABLY

Despite our claims to perfection, walking on the water still proves difficult for most entrepreneurs. Most of us still get our ankles wet occasionally. All of us need a few "tricks of the trade" to use when managing by the book just doesn't work.

When my husband and I first worked out a "split shift" working arrangement, I learned just how useful tricks of the trade can be. On Mondays, Wednesdays and Fridays he left work early to be home to greet our daughter when she arrived home from school. On Tuesdays and Thursdays, I did. All parties involved were pleased. No day care was required. I cheerfully left the office at the appointed time with a loaded briefcase and set up shop in my home office in the afternoons. Doesn't this sound like utopia for the working parent? Hardly. The office staff quickly became familiar with my schedule, and it soon became obvious there was a down side to our perfect parenting schedule.

I quickly discovered that the moment I was out the door, certain employees all but ceased working. Other employees continued to forge ahead but occasionally roared down the wrong road in the absence of managerial direction. These two very different responses made me realize that two distinct types of individuals worked for the company and that each had different managerial needs.

Those who forged ahead remained productive, regardless of who was watching. Their sense of commitment stemmed from personal drive that caused them to do their best regardless of their audience. For these individuals, they themselves set the height of the bar. Excellence for them was a personal desire, not a corporate response. The other group, whose productivity ground to a halt when I was not in the office, reacted solely to their environment. They responded to a measurement system applied by outsiders that included bosses, spouses, friends and even children. If someone of importance was not around to witness an event, they believed the event in question "didn't count."

Internally driven employees are far easier to cope with from a management perspective. They "catch the dust as it falls." They take pride in anticipating problems and in solving them while they are still in their infancy. Often, they are entrepreneurial themselves. They just don't possess the full suite of talents to allow them to attain the escape velocity necessary to strike out on their own. If anything needs to be done with people of this type, it is to rein them in. Driving them would be redundant. They are by definition, driven.

The other group presents more challenges. Managing them demands that you hone your parenting skills to a fine art. They set their watches to synchronize precisely with your arrival and departure time. They expend significant energy to insure that you see them working hard and that you don't see them when they are slacking off.

With this dichotomy of personnel, how do you address the need to micro-manage without insulting the intelligence (and worse yet, quell the initiative) of those who are internally driven? You use the "call in, call often, call unpredictably," method of management.

Surprisingly enough, it is quite effective with both types of individuals. For those whose gratification comes from their environment (that means you) they are supplied with motivation to keep working in your absence. This is because your frequent calls give them the opportunity to regale you with accomplishments they completed in your absence, apprise you of situations that may require your attention (a form of oddly useful whistle blowing), and prove, since they are answering the phone, that they are still in the office. They soon learn that a lack of physical presence does not mean a lack of managerial presence. Yes, the workday does in fact continue after the boss walks out the door.

There are also ways to enhance the effectiveness of your calls. Make sure that those who work only when they are environmentally challenged have concrete projects they can perform in your absence and that the time frames they have been given to complete their projects are finite. This way you can call and ask for a status report on a particular project. "Andy, are you on track to get that proposal out in FedEx tonight? That package must be in their hands tomorrow so any log jam that could prevent this from happening must be cleared today."

"Oh, by the way," comments are also effective. "Oh, by the way Jamie, I have a meeting in the morning and I need that cash flow analysis on my desk by 9:00 a.m. tomorrow. I just wanted to call you early enough this afternoon to make sure you have time to finish it. If you have any questions, call me at my home office." These calls send a singular message. Work is continuing as usual. Nothing has changed but my location. You are still being managed. Even though it is remote management, I still am going to keep tabs on what you are doing.

Is it as good as being in the office? No. Playtime will still occur. Chatting will proceed unbridled, but at least circumstances will limit it to some degree. It will stop long enough for Andy to get the package for FedEx prepared and Jamie will sigh a bit, yet buckle down to get the cash flow done before she leaves.

Impromptu calling works for the driven group for different reasons. This group is always seeking answers. In fact, they are often irritated by your absence because they find their progress slowed when they are unable to get a response from you that would allow them to forge ahead. When you call in unpredictably, they frequently ask for decisions or input, or ask you to remove roadblocks they have encountered. People in this group also appreciate the opportunity to get the warm-fuzzies that calling in typically provides. They too, enjoy getting the bosses ear to share progress made on recent assignments so that in return, they can receive accolades that go with a job well done.

It is healthy to acknowledge that we are all human and frequently cannot attain every lofty management goal to which we aspire, like perfectly motivating every employee within the company. Sometimes the best approach is to simply employ a trick or two (like calling in when you can't be in the office) to shore up the business on those days when you don't quite manage by the book.

CHAPTER THIRTY-SIX

THE POWER OF THE POTLUCK

Once in a while, when the mood strikes, someone suggests a company potluck. When this occurs, we turn the conference table into a big buffet and everyone grazes for several hours. Things seem a little less urgent when you are munching hot wings, discussing people's food allergies, problems with children, vehicle preferences, and most embarrassing moments. Supplanting the normal office banter occasionally, causes everyone to breathe a collective sigh of relief.

Although I have consistently trashed the idea of corporate getaways, I have found there is much to recommend the potluck.

There is no hidden meaning behind the potluck. People don't waste time analyzing it to death to decide if it is a real corporate benefit. They simply enjoy it and let their hair down. Even the human side of entrepreneurs comes out during these impromptu encounters, and best of all, it lowers the corporate blood pressure dramatically.

We also decree Pizza Day at the office now and then. On these days, the company buys pizza for the whole office, and everyone sits down and eats together. Although this is appreciated by the staff, it is not as good as the potluck because the "company-paid lunch" some-how takes part of the comradery away. It is the contribution of every-one, regardless of rank, that makes the potluck so special.

In order to get potlucks started at your office, go to the morale leader (the person who instigates birthday parties and drives everyone nuts with ideas for corporate bonding) and mention to her that you think it would be great if someone suggested having a potluck. Hopefully, she will step up to the plate to organize it and all you will have to do is to sign up to bring something on the appropriate day.

Potlucks are wonderful because:

1. They de-stress the office.

2. You get a bird's eye view of employees interacting socially, which can be quite helpful in ironing out the people problems in your company.

3. They sometimes let you build emotional bridges to your employees on a one-to-one basis.

4. They tend to break down barriers between supervisors and reportees.

5. They make weight gain the subject of the day instead of who is doing what to whom.

6. They are free and any time lost is inconsequential, particularly after factoring in improved morale.

7. They are fun and the food is typically pretty good.

Life is too short. No one needs to learn this lesson more than the typical type A, overachiever entrepreneur. Take the time and plan a potluck and experience the ultimate in casual, corporate dining. It's good for everyone's mental health!

MANAGEMENT MAGIC

CHAPTER THIRTY-SEVEN

REVEAL EMPLOYEE CREATIVITY — ABOLISH THE DRESS CODE

Creative thinking is not a question of intelligence, it is a question of motivation. Motivated people are the ones who strive to find solutions. As a business owner, the trick is to motivate. Creative thinking will result.

Several years ago, I was convinced our employees lacked creativity. It seemed every "spark" required to dream up a new product or solve a tough problem came from me.

I changed my mind. The day we abolished the formal dress code in favor of "business casual" I learned just how creative our employees could be. I discovered that certain employees, with the help of creative interpretation, now considered cutoffs, sandals, tank tops and see-through blouses to be in line with the dress code. People thought of all sorts of ways to make their favorite apparel permissible. They compared our dress code to that of other companies. They invested in new, better looking jeans. They went to great lengths to make sure I didn't see them when they were wearing something iffy. It made *me* think. "Why don't they put this much creative energy into what they normally do?"

Finally the light came on. Clothing is important because recognition is important. It lets us communicate our personality to others and is a badge that links us to social groups and belief systems. What we choose to wear creates in us a sense of belonging and security. I began to focus on ways to meet those same psychological needs without the benefit of jeans with the knees missing.

I decided it was time to go back to basics and resurrect recognition as a not so secret, motivational weapon. Now I deploy it at every opportunity. The best opportunities are frequently our regularly scheduled company meetings.

Three times a week we have an operations meeting. In that meeting I use praise sparingly, but often with humor to maximize its impact. "Sarah, since you came up with that idea to prevent production errors, we will now have to refer to you as Queen of Quality Control. From now on, all employees will bow discreetly when they see you in the hall." Or, "Bob, do you know what your idea means to the company? Your idea will save $4,000 a month, more than enough to pay someone's salary. Ideas like that keep us in business."

When I praise someone, it's more than just "nice job." I want them to see the significance of their acts. I want their peers to see the significance. Most of all, I want them to feel good about what they did and remember that feeling a long time. Remembering will motivate. It will cause them to repeat the behavior in the future.

It is recognition that sparks creativity in your employees and makes them great contributors to your business. Take every opportunity to recognize individual contributions. Collective creativity is ultimately what will make your business a success.

CHAPTER THIRTY-EIGHT

MIDDLE MANAGEMENT— THE SOURCE OF ALL POLITICS

Middle managers do not do, and they do not decide. They are, for the most part, conduits that both those above and below see as obstacles to getting things done. As a result, middle managers often get no real sense of accomplishment. The credit for corporate decisions is taken by senior management while credit for completed work is taken by those in the trenches.

At some point, usually during a belt tightening episode or some other reorganization, the value of middle managers is measured anew. This reevaluation of their usefulness is an ever-present threat, so that even the densest of middle managers perceives the need to insure their future by raising their worth in relation to their peers.

If this were not enough, the pyramid management structure of most businesses pretty well guarantees that career path opportunities will be bestowed on only a select few and that termination or at best, stagnation is in store for the remainder.

So how do these middle managers respond to their environment? Just as you would expect. They knife, claw, position, gossip, attempt power plays, and conduct "relationship building" with higher ups. They try to increase their group's head count, find fault with peers, attempt to remain visible, look for mentors, identify scapegoats, attempt to become favorites, and try to be viewed as indispensable.

No deep analysis is required here. Left unbridled, this type of behavior tears a business apart, and productivity all but grinds to a halt. So rather than belabor the damage that is done, here is how to solve the problem.

Keep middle managers busy with real work. Real work is defined as something that produces a product, directly relates to supporting customers or prospective customers, or involves a task that is required to directly meet outside obligations of the business. Work is not writing memos, meeting with others in the company, preparing schedules, engaging in planning, morale building, organizing, or systematizing. It is never managing personnel.

I don't care how many reportees a manager may have, they must have a healthy share (at least fifty percent of their time) allocated to responsibilities that require them to use their own skills.

Having direct responsibilities results in many positives. First, managers now get a sense of personal accomplishment as the results of their efforts move the business forward in real, measurable ways. Doing real work also sets a good example for reportees which helps build appreciation and respect among the ranks for management overall. Next, hands-on tasks also help managers keep their hands in departmental operations, which supplies them with knowledge that improves their managerial decisions. Finally, real work means less discretionary time. Whoever said, "Idle hands are the devils workshop," was right on the mark.

As you begin to assign real work to managers, an amazing thing happens. You find out that certain managers can't or are too lazy to do work directly. Guess what? These are the ones you fire! The weeding out process has been done for you because it goes without saying that in every organization there is management deadwood that desperately needs to be identified and removed.

Obviously, it is necessary to maintain some sort of middle management structure in larger organizations to insure corporate priorities are conveyed and achievements are monitored. The key is to make it efficient.

Spend some time giving serious thought to the type of direct work assignments you could give your management team, and then make those assignments. The ones that walk out over it needed to leave anyway, and you will find their exodus and the new found sense of accomplishment burgeoning in those that remain, to be a very sweet and profitable reward for both you and your employees.

Chapter Thirty-Nine

No More Mr. Nice Guy

Over the last fifty years employment has changed from a permanent relationship into a transient one. Many people you hire, while believing they must stay employed, also understand that they do not have to stay employed by *you* and treat the job accordingly.

Typically, employees feel entitled to be humored, nurtured, and protected. They expect health care, sick days, paid vacation, time off for funerals of friends and distant relations, family reunions and a host of holidays.

In this world of entitlements, it is hard to encourage people to contribute as our parents once did. The work ethic they knew belongs to a bygone era. What is easy to find today is an extremely healthy ego and abundant pride in self that makes an employee care deeply about what his or her peers think.

Knowing about the importance of pride however, supplies the entrepreneur with the ultimate managerial weapon, embarrassment. By using this method, you can get employees, who view work as an entitlement and fail to respond to kinder management techniques, to put their nose to the grindstone permanently!

Allen was manager of operations. Whenever he was asked about a project, the answer was always a blank stare and "I don't know." Finally, my patience gave way. I looked at him squarely in the eye. "Aren't you the one who logs the data? I would think you would know where we stand. We will wait so you can go look it up right now." And with that, he was dismissed from the room. All eight people watched in silence as he got up from his chair. Did I yell? No. Did I threaten? No. Did I embarrass the pants off him? You betcha! Did he ever fail to keep track of logged data after that meeting? Hardly.

One day we ran out of paper printed with a custom client logo and were unable to finish a print run (a disaster for a billing company). I narrowed my focus to the persons in charge of ordering and inventory. "I thought we had an inventory procedure that prevented this from happening. Who checked the inventory for this billing?" I knew the answer to my question before I asked it. Squirming ensued while I let a very, very long moment of silence descend upon the room. Inventory never seemed to be a problem again.

My goal is to prevent repetition of mistakes by making the infraction painful enough to the ego of the offender to insure he or she will take great pains to see it doesn't happen again.

And what is the downside of all of this? The weak hearted and generally incompetent people will quit. The marginal ones will improve. The good ones will NEVER DO IT AGAIN. Not a bad outcome.

Of all the suggestions contained in this book however, this one comes with the most caveats. You must know when and how to do this or it will blow up in your face. You must always deal your blows uniformly and equitably. If you fail to do so, you will lose credibility, and once this is gone, so is your authority.

Here is when you should *not* use this method. Never embarrass when a legitimate problem needs to be solved. If we did not have an inventory system, or if there was any doubt at all that the system, not the person, might be the problem, I would have followed standard problem solving procedures. Embarrassment should be reserved for solving difficult behavioral problems, not business issues. Also, do not use this method on a first offense. Recognize that management by embarrassment constitutes bringing out the heavy artillery and should clearly be saved for repeat offenders.

It is often effective to merely mention to a supervisor that if his reportee fails to respond appropriately in the future, management by embarrassment will be your weapon of choice, and he is free to warn his reportee of this fact. Usually this instantly results in a closed-door session and the problem frequently never surfaces again. Having your reputation precede you can be a good thing.

Before you apply this method, here is the biggest caveat of all. Make sure you have all the facts before you strike. If there is any legitimate reason why someone failed to do something, you've had it. Your behavior will then be viewed as unfair and tyrannical, and you will lose the respect of your organization.

Do not let me scare you away from using this tool, just use it judiciously. It will solve behavioral problems that can be solved no other way.

CHAPTER FORTY

INITIALS—
THE PRIDE OF DOING

We have all experienced buying a pair of jeans or other article of clothing, sticking our hand in the pocket, and extracting a little piece of paper that says, Inspected by Sally, Rose, Edwardo... you fill in the blank. It always causes me to conjure up the face of a person, mindlessly, hour after hour, adding that little piece of paper to everything they inspect.

What's the point? Will I ever meet Sally? No. Will I ever know the person behind the name? No. Will Sally be a better inspector because I am holding that little piece of paper in my hand? Of course. Pride in what we do is universal. Why do painters sign their work? Why don't authors publish anonymously? Why do imprints of feet immortalized in cement rank as a crowning achievement to most stars? Pride may be a sin, but deadly or not, it's one of the emotions that makes us go.

For years our company had an operations check sheet that outlined every step in our monthly billing process. Next to each step listed was a box to record the date and time each was completed. The form got filled out, but amazingly the tasks marked as complete, often were not. We sat down with the operators who were responsible for filling out the form. They said they were too busy to fill out the form. They said they sometimes missed steps because they had to go back and fill the

125

form out after processing was complete. They said they "thought" the step was done when they marked the sheet. They blamed each other for filling in erroneous information. Often, we heard that good ol' standby, "That's not *my* writing." The excuses were endless.

Why couldn't we get a grip on this simple task? Because there was no accountability; there was no pride of authorship. It was just part of a job, and worse yet, it was a shared job because one operator passed the responsibility for continuing to another operator at the conclusion of his shift. We thought long and hard about this problem and put in a very sophisticated and costly solution. We added one more column to our Excel spread sheet and put "Initials" at the top.

You would have thought we had dropped an atom bomb on the computer center. Everyone was aghast. Some considered this new procedure akin to being watched electronically by Big Brother. People would know *who* did the work and when. They would be accountable. They could no longer hide behind the warm, protective cloak of anonymity.

The bell had rung. The game had begun. I could now ask, "Adam, why did you initial the step showing the revenue report had been run? The files needed as input to that report have not been generated yet." This was the first in a long list of questions. I smiled. They didn't. A flurry of resignations followed. Well, if you can't take the heat, get out of the kitchen, works. Our kitchen was now manned by a somber and small (but competent and emotionally secure) operations staff.

From that day on, the number of mistakes dropped like a stone. Those who stayed maintained a strong commitment to doing things right and showed they clearly understood what constituted a job well done. They were delighted to fill in their initials because they were proud of what they had accomplished and wanted someone to overtly appreciate their efforts. To the successful operators, accountability was fraught with rewards.

What we had inadvertently done with our little initialing system was to improve the quality of our staff by producing a self-correcting system of employment. I was dumbfounded, but happy.

The clients now received a better product in less time and best of all, the 110-decibel grumbling ceased. With the exodus of the shirkers, everybody worked. Life was good.

I now smile every time I see the words, Inspected by Sally. I envision a room full of people who care enough to put their name on what they do. What they do *does* matter. It's not just a question of who sees the tag.

If a tree falls in the forest and there is no one to hear the crash, does it make any noise? You betcha. It is important to the tree that it fell, and the label, that no one may ever see, is important to Sally.

Chapter Forty-One

The Magic Paper Trail

In business, those who survive are not always the fittest, more often they are the ones who maintain the best documentation. Every court case, personnel hearing, patent challenge, or contract dispute centers around documentation.

For years I have been preaching to my employees to *write it down*. My employees have consistently ignored these sermons. Getting my staff to document is like trying to get my daughter to do something while she is watching Cartoon Network. She (and they) display selective deafness. There is a difference between the two, however. My daughter doesn't even bother to acknowledge my presence in the room. My employees actually respond and then ignore me. This shows I have hired well. They have all refined their skills in business etiquette.

For a long time I could not figure out why people refused to document things when the benefits to the business were so obvious. It finally dawned on me that "benefits to the business" was the key. The benefits derived from documentation go primarily to the owner of the business, not to the employee charged with recording the event.

If a contract dispute ensues years later, will the customer service representative (CSR) do battle with client management over what did or did not occur? Will she pay the legal fees or lose money as a result of a negative outcome in a contract dispute? No. Only her boss will. It's human nature to only care about the things that impact us directly.

Perhaps you are thinking that there *are* benefits that accrue to the CSR from documentation. Documenting customer exchanges keeps both parties organized, clarifies commitments and removes confusion between representatives and the customers they support. All these things are true, but I will tell you that despite these obvious advantages, there is not a CSR alive who will voluntarily document his calls. The benefits to the CSR are inadequate to establish the sense of ownership needed to drive documentation, yet the overwhelming benefits to the entrepreneur make his need to document, an obsession.

How then, do we get employees to document? How do we make the magic paper trail benefit them to a greater degree? We dangle the ultimate carrot and make the benefit of documenting the retention of one's job. Insuring the continued success of the business years hence is a nebulous concept and one that is unimportant to most employees. Most of the people you currently employ will not even work for you three years from now. Send them a message that is short and sweet. You want to remain employed? Write it down. It's that simple. That's a benefit everyone can relate to.

Establishing and maintaining a good paper trail is probably one of the hardest things you will ever try to implement in your business. Unfortunately, it is also one of the most important.

Start by requiring that communications between your employees and your clients be in writing. The pervasive use of e-mail in the last decade has provided us with a painless way to document what is being said. Next, expand the benefits of e-mail by requiring employees to produce follow-up e-mails, which document telephone conversations as well. You can easily police the use of this system by requiring all employees to bcc (blind carbon copy) you on every e-mail sent.

Finally, in order to insure that you do not lose the e-mails that serve as your only documentation, you will need to have a way to centrally store and organize them. One easy way to do this is to set up an e-mail address on your server for each client or client category and have everyone send a copy of every client e-mail to this additional address. In turn, if the e-mail is incoming, simply have the recipient forward the e-mail to this new address. Now the search becomes easier. There is only one place to look, and that place has information organized by client or client group. If you also require meaningful titles to be entered for each e-mail, you have it made. It's easy. Virtually no extra time is required to perform the archive function and the problem of backing up data is solved. By placing a copy of everything on the server, your system administrator (who may be you) can make sure the client e-mail directories are backed up on a regular basis.

Little mishaps are inevitable. On numerous occasions, I have found that the e-mail documentation I was *positive* we had no longer existed because it had been purged, lost, or deleted because someone "didn't know" it was important. To protect yourself against the inevitable, here is a summary of the golden rules of documentation. Take them to heart and do not underestimate how important enforcing these rules can be to your business.

All employees should be required to comply with the following rules:

1. All business requests and responses must be made via e-mail.

2. All phone conversations containing requests or responses must be followed up with a clarifying e-mail.

3. No e-mail correspondence may be deleted without express permission from you or a supervisor you designate.

4. All e-mail correspondence is to be sent to other client support representatives supporting the same client group as blind carbon copies (bcc).

5. All e-mail correspondence is to be sent to the appropriate manager and you, the owner. If you have a large group of CSRs, create a second e-mail address for yourself and have them e-mail to this second address to prevent overwhelming your regular e-mail account.

6. Require all employees to send copies to single client e-mail addresses or client groups, located on your server. Back up that server on a regular basis.

7. Require all your employees to adequately title their e-mails to allow you to quickly identify both the customer and the subject without opening the e-mail.

Compliance with an e-mail procedure is a work in progress. You will never get 100 percent compliance nor alleviate the grumbling and whining that accompanies enforcing a policy that your employees view as overhead. Just accept the fact and put up with it. The next time you are in court doing battle, loaded to the teeth with documentation, it will all seem worth the effort.

FATHERLY ADVICE

CHAPTER FORTY-TWO

SIX KITTENS AND A CAR

My father told me this joke a long time ago. I think the practical implications for business are self-evident and well worth repeating.

One day a man was driving along when he spotted a car stuck in the mud by the side of the road. He pulled over to help and was amazed by what he saw. The driver was trying to tie six kittens to the car's front bumper with a rope. "You don't really think those six kittens can pull a 2,000 pound car out of the mud do you?" the man asked. "Why not?" the driver replied, "I've got a whip."

Entrepreneurs often forget there are only supposed to be eight hours in a workday. If employees don't achieve balance between work and home life, they will quit.

It is also important to remember *no one* will work as hard for you as you will. Don't delude yourself. Even if you think you have your employees in golden handcuffs because of high unemployment or some other proverbial whip, employees still vote with their feet, regardless of circumstance.

"Because I'm the boss and I said so," does not work any better than, "Because I'm the mom and I said so." Always remember that to be successful at retaining employees you must be persuasive, not dictatorial.

Chapter Forty-Three

Count Your Near Misses

When I was sixteen, my father sat me down to have a serious talk about driving. This occurred immediately following my first "on road" experience, during which, he stated, "You have been driving for ten minutes. Based upon the duration of your driving career I think fifty miles an hour is excessive." Okay, I have always had a reputation for pushing the envelope a bit, but hey, all sixteen-year-olds like to live on the edge.

When you're young and foolish, living on the edge can be exciting. In business living on the edge simply means you are working without a net. You have increased your chances of failure by increasing your businesses' vulnerability. It is only a question of time before you fall.

Does your business live on the edge? It is not difficult to tell.

One day during a heated discussion about the latest operational screw-up that had occurred, I said through my teeth, "We spend more time fixing mistakes than we do running normal production!" Fortunately, at that moment, I was actually listening to my own tirade. "Oooooh!" I said, "Watson, I think I've got it! We put all our energy into fixing things. Too bad we don't put the same energy into preventing the mistakes in the first place."

We all sat around looking at each other in silence. An ultimate truth had been spoken and we all knew it. For the first time in months, humility prevailed. "Perhaps we need to focus on our near misses," I said.

I returned to the wisdom of my father. "When I was learning how to drive," I told the group, "my father told me to evaluate my driving skill by counting how many near misses I had. If I routinely performed panic stops, I needed to slow down. If I often found myself barely squeaking back into line after passing a car, I needed to allow a greater passing distance to add a margin of safety." "If you make these adjustments," he said, "you will not only reduce your near misses, you will reduce your number of accidents. Near misses are a matter of skill. Accidents are a matter of luck."

I looked at the group. "Our luck hasn't been very good lately," I said. "I suggest we work on improving our skills instead." That meeting launched a campaign to examine virtually every system we employed, as we looked for ways to add a critical margin of safety. It soon became obvious that the skills we needed to acquire were those needed to improve quality control.

We began by counting our near misses to determine which areas were the most vulnerable. Any time anyone discovered a problem, even if it was corrected before it became customer-affecting, we counted it as a near miss. It did not take long before the statistics we gathered were screaming the answers we sought. We knew exactly where we were the weakest and aggressively took steps to plug the holes.

The return on the time we spent counting near misses was staggering. In less than thirty days, we had done over a dozen things to stop the "accidents." As my father used to tell me, "You ought to listen to the old and bald." Okay, Dad, you win. And by listening to you, we all win.

CHAPTER FORTY-FOUR

WHY DAD IS SMARTER THAN YOU ARE

We all acknowledge that the intelligence of parents increases dramatically between the time we begin educating them (sometime during our adolescence) and the time we finish up the process, ten years later.

Once we view them as able to supply us with assistance outside the financial realm, it is frightening to discover that the advice they foist upon us is, for the most part, pretty good.

Sometimes asking for advice is like unleashing a dragon, and the conversation often ends with a hurt look and the statement, "Well, you *did* ask for my advice, didn't you?" This is understandable however, for much of their advice is pent up, stemming from the period when they were forced to bite their tongues over halter tops, tattoos, body piercing and questionable associates, as their educators aged from fourteen to twenty.

My father, the GGBA (Great Giver of Benevolent Advice), always referred to advising as "steering." He often explained to me that he received great satisfaction from watching the progress I made as he steered me (with my occasional help) around the little obstacles of business. He frequently reminded me he was quite comfortable in taking 100 percent of the credit for all my worthwhile accomplishments.

We padded along for a number of years in our respective roles as advisor and advisee, solving the little lamentations of the business as they occurred. One day the problem wasn't so little. We had lost a number of clients in a short period of time, due to a myriad of circumstances, and simply did not have the critical mass to keep going. I could not pay myself. The company was already operating with a skeleton crew. I told my father it was time to give up.

At the time the business had been operating for five years. We had weathered a number of crises, yet always before, I could see light at the end of the tunnel. If I failed to see a solution, often someone else in the company could see some glimmer and we all worked together to resolve our plight. This time there was no light, and no one, not even my GGBA, had any suggestions.

Understanding the importance of remaining a leader under all conditions, I still led the charge at the office, but inside I had given up. I had no answers. For the first time that I could remember, my father did not have any solutions either. He did however, have some advice. His advice was to do nothing.

This advice really went against my grain. Do nothing, definitely didn't work for me. Was he having a "senior" moment?

"Look," he said, "If you elect to fold the business and get a job working for somebody else, what happens? You start sending out resumes and looking for a job. You wouldn't do that right before Christmas in any event. The timing's just bad. Also, although many companies seem to have a penchant for letting people go right before Christmas, I know that's not your style. You're not going to do that either. So do nothing. Wait a couple of weeks and see if anything is different. You don't have to make the decision to close the business right now." As usual, he was right.

I took a deep breath. Why did I need him to simply restate the obvious? Because I was standing in the middle of the problem and it wasn't obvious to me. I could make the announcement, but what for? Why wreck the holidays for myself and everyone else?

Upon returning to work after New Years, we got a call from a company we had been courting for six months. "I'm finally ready to get going," he said. "It's the start of the new year and I thought to myself, I bet those people think I fell off the planet, after taking half the year to make a decision!"

His call did more than tell us we had a new client. To me, it was an omen that perhaps the tide was turning. We hadn't talked to Allen for months because we were convinced he would never make a decision. But good ol' Allen just had his troubles like everyone else. At the time I thought Allen saved the company. He didn't. Someone older and wiser did. Someone who had the wisdom, the experience, and the objectivity to say, "Do nothing."

Don't discount parental advice merely out of habit. If your parents are willing to share their wisdom and experience, take the time to listen. Their objectivity, desire to help, and knowledge of you, can make their advice better than any consultant's.

CHAPTER FORTY-FIVE

LET PEOPLE QUIT

There are a few basic tenets of business that should never be violated. Do not hire relatives tops the list, but not far below is another rule: When someone quits, LET THEM GO.

Even Robert Half, king of employment agencies supports this one. According to Robert, almost all employees who resign and are then coerced, cajoled, or bribed into staying, are gone a year later.

You may think that making concessions to retain employees is a small price to pay to keep knowledge from walking out the door. Any teacher can tell you the price is never small. One unruly child always disrupts the entire class. Work is just a classroom of children who get paid to be there.

Early in my career, I frequently made the mistake of trying to retain "indispensable" employees. I stopped when my father told me about the ten percent rule.

One day as I was blowing a gasket over someone's sudden resignation, my father, who still treated me as a five-year-old when he wished to dictate, shut me down. "You are not acknowledging the ten percent rule," he said. "WHATEVER!" I shouted. I was on a roll and was enjoying lambasting my recently departed employee. I wanted to savor the moment. "Be quiet you little beast," he said with a fatherly license that allowed interruption, "and I'll tell you why."

141

I was irritated over not being allowed to vent, but I stopped talking, like a good five-year-old. "An unhappy employee takes ten percent off everyone they work with. You're an accountant," he said. "Do the math."

"Does he never tire of being right?" I thought irritably. His raised eyebrow and the glint in his eye told me he was not the least bit tired of it. I begrudgingly realized I had just heard one of the great truths of business.

Since then, experience has taught me there are many reasons behind the rule. Not only do concessions seldom work, they are *always* expensive. Trying to keep a quitter from leaving seldom works because the feeling underlying the reason they wanted to quit does not go away. If they felt under-appreciated or under-compensated, the feeling generally remains even if the causative factor is actually removed. A disgruntled employee is like the bad apple in the barrel. Her negativity will spread throughout the organization like a cancer, and, in most cases, the damage she causes will go undetected until morale within the company is lower than _____. (Fill in whatever term you find politically correct.)

Once we employed a programmer named Jenny. We tolerated her grumbles of dissatisfaction month after month. We humored her with a nice office, flextime, and gave her latitude to design programs that her level of talent did not warrant. She decided to quit. We begged her to stay because she was the only one who knew how to work on certain programs and we were scared to be without anyone who could do her function, even temporarily.

Here was the problem. She really wanted to orchestrate, not program. She said she needed more autonomy, but what she wanted was less work. So when we gave her the autonomy she asked for and more money to boot, it didn't matter. In her mind, nothing had really changed. She still didn't have what she wanted. Because she had made her speech and had gotten what she asked for however, she had to stick around to save face. As soon as she found a way to re-justify her decision to leave, she was gone.

While she was searching for a reason, she bad-mouthed everyone and everything in the company and did only a minimal amount of work. She left three months later but only after she had destroyed the morale and reduced the productivity (by at *least* ten percent) of everyone with whom she worked. We were shocked and confused. Why did she leave? Didn't we do everything she asked? Yes, and *asked* is the operative word. We did what she asked but not what she wanted.

Don't hyperventilate over resignations. Statistically, very few of those you convince to stay will stick anyway. Just buy them a cake, collect their keys and move on. Once you do the math, the ten percent rule will make the decision to let them go, an easy one.

Chapter Forty-Six

What Were You Doing?
Just Spitting

During the 1960's my father was plant manager for a chemical company in Buffalo, N.Y. The entire system was automated and possessed sophisticated controls for the production of acid.

One morning my father headed toward his office, which required him to walk through the center of the factory. Something caught his eye as he walked past. About 100 feet in the air sat a man on a catwalk (a high, narrow, exposed walkway suspended in the air). To make matters worse, an exposed river of acid flowed by that point in open piping. Dad was appalled. He quickly climbed the barrel ladder up to the spot and immediately recognized the man as one of the day operators who was not scheduled to begin work for another hour.

"Gee Joe, what are you doing up here? It's dangerous! OSHA would have a fit if they saw you!" "I'm spitting," was Joe's reply. "You see, you youngsters don't remember, but in the old days this is how we did it. You can tell by the hiss that we're doing fine. Here, just listen." And with that he spit into the acid that was roaring by. The hiss, which was caused by the reaction between the water and the acid, quickly subsided.

"That's all very interesting, but we don't need to spit anymore. Everything is electronically controlled." "Oh, yes we do," Joe said. "Last night those electronic controls you youngsters love so much went out, just before my shift was over. I know how important it is to you to keep this place running, so I decided I wouldn't mind sitting up here awhile and spitting to keep things going right." Just then he spit and in response to the hiss, carefully adjusted the big water intake valve on the system. "Nobody's used this valve in years, but it still works," he said smiling.

Dad had to smile too. Shutting down the process would have cost the company $10,000 an hour, and Joe had been there from 4:00 p.m. to almost 6:00 a.m. Fourteen hours, or more importantly, $140,000 later. "It's still awful dangerous Joe," my father said. "Not for me it isn't," Joe said. "Besides, I really wanted to help you out. You're the only guy in this place who gives a damn about what the operators think and you always do what you can to help us out. I just wanted to return the favor." "Well," said Dad, "let me get the maintenance crew to fix the controls, but if you wouldn't mind, I'd sure appreciate it if you would keep us on-line until the repairs are done."

An hour later Joe was heading home feeling he had really accomplished something and my father was finally making his way to his office. Why did Joe exhibit exceptional loyalty? Because he was treated as an equal. Showing respect for those who work for you is a simple thing to do. It is also the key to successful management.

What did my father do to make Joe believe he considered him an equal worthy of respect? First, he listened. He didn't leap to conclusions or begin the conversation by assuming he understood the situation. Instead, he collected all the facts and then showed gratitude to Joe for his initiative, even when that initiative was somewhat misguided. Finally he rewarded those actions that displayed characteristics he sought to encourage, like Joe's desire to help solve the problem of keeping the factory running, despite the obvious liability and endangerment issues his actions created.

In short, Dad always remembered the golden rule: "Do unto others as you would have them do unto you." He did not give it lip service; he lived by it and in so doing, his respect for others came across in everything he did, and he received respect in return.

Whenever I hire someone, I try to convey that in our company, we respect one another, not for our titles but for what we can do to lighten each other's load. I make a point to explain the only difference between various employees in the company is their level of risk, and I try to live by that rule.

Next time you are tempted to react to a situation because an employee did not act as you would have in a similar situation, stop and try to walk a mile in his moccasins. Were his motives good? Did he act in a manner consistent with his skill set and knowledge base for the good of the company? If he did, bite your tongue, appreciate his purest of motives, and accept his actions graciously as a gift. After all, no one can demand respect; it must be given freely. If you are lucky enough to be given that gift, make sure your employee knows you are grateful.

Chapter Forty-Seven

If It's Free
And Reversible, Do It

Many people considered my father a genius. Not the lofty or eccentric kind, but a creative genius who could see solutions to problems that routinely baffled others. I used to tell him that his forte was his ability to be "creative on demand." He could focus on a problem to the exclusion of all else, and bingo! out came a solution, just like clockwork.

Having a quick mind however, certainly had its down side. It made him impatient with others who laboriously slugged through exercises to solve problems which, he felt, had obvious solutions. Occasionally he would share stories from work which had particularly taxed his patience.

Early in his career he worked for a large chemical company. He shared a big office with fifty other engineers who all shared the support services of a secretarial pool. At one end of the room were the secretaries and at the other end were the file cabinets.

One of the secretaries requested that the file cabinets be relocated to the other end of the room where she and the other secretaries could easily access them. To support her case, she noted that she made, on average, forty trips across the room each day just to use the files.

Her boss listened patiently. He said he would review her request and get back to her the next week. When she inquired again, two weeks later, her boss said he had not had time to look into it, but assured her it was a top priority and that he would get her an answer shortly. Three months later, Gracie tendered her resignation, much to the shock and dismay of her boss who didn't understand why she was leaving.

My father came home livid. He felt she was the most competent secretary in the pool. I remember him referring to Gracie's boss and his fellow managers as "a bunch of morons." That night after dinner, Dad said, "Marsha, I'm going to give you a rule you can use to make decisions that those morons at the office clearly don't get. If you're faced with a decision, evaluate it on the spot. If whatever is being requested can be put back, doesn't cost any money, and is not dangerous or discriminatory, the answer is yes. It's a non-decision. Moving those file cabinets would not have cost the company a cent. If it didn't work out they could be put back for free. But the price they've paid now is the cost of losing the best secretary the engineering department ever had."

I don't know if I remembered the rule so well because it seemed logical at the time or because my father's anger over the incident made the rule memorable. I do know that over the life of my career it has turned out to be one of the most useful and time saving suggestions he ever gave me.

When people come up to me with a request, I just spout the rule, and if their request passes the test, they are free to do whatever it is they want to do. Believe me, if it needs to be reversed, it quickly becomes apparent. I try to get those who direct others to apply this same rule and save their decision-making authority for the important stuff.

If you are a busy manager, "the rule" is really the gift that keeps on giving. The gift of a quick answer not only benefits those who make requests, it also benefits those who grant requests. As a request grantor, you will benefit from happier employees and a more productive workplace.

Applying this simple little rule can help turn you into a boss who cares enough to listen. Sometimes what is important to do is actually easy to do. Sometimes all it takes is a nod and a smile.

SECRET WEAPONS

CHAPTER FORTY-EIGHT

MAKING A LIST AND CHECKING IT TWICE

Here is my number one, super fantastic, key to the city, secret to success. Make a list. Do it every day. Do it before you do anything else. Refer to it all day long.

It is my secret weapon to productivity. It allows me to do three times the work of most people. Why? Because most people do what they like to do first, instead of what they need to do.

I have perfected my list making over the years and have found that how you make your list can be as important as having a list. Rule number one. Do not use a computer. First, a computer is not impromptu. You don't always have it available when you want to add something. Frequently, by the time you get to where you can add something, you forget it. This includes small laptop computers as well. They still have to be turned on and the proper entry screen needs to be selected. Computers are also far too complicated to be successful. This is why Palm Pilots don't work either.

Ten years ago, I got a Sharp Wizard electronic organizer. It allowed me to enter everything by typing on its itty bitty keyboard. I loved my Wizard. It was my friend and I carried it everywhere. I started out by entering a couple of dozen items in it. Slowly that number increased, as I realized my Sharp Wizard had lots of memory! I could keep on adding things without ever having to delete anything. It got a bit

151

laborious to scroll through my roughly 150 items, but hey, I might actually get to some of those "B list" items some day. Each morning I would get up and open my Wizard. I scrolled through the list, carefully adding anything I thought might be nice to do in the next hundred years. So what if my little morning exercise now took forty-five minutes to do? I was organized! I was electronic.

I did realize however, that I had a problem. I could not segregate my lists into the today list, the maybe today list, the this week list, the maybe this month list and the hopefully I'll get around to it someday list. I needed more power.

I did my research and I was ready to buy. I needed a Sharp OZ 9600 Model II. What an awesome model! I could check mark things as done; I could do multiple lists; I could sort my lists and search using key words; I could type on the itty bitty keyboard that was laid out like a real keyboard. Life was GOOD! I hardly noticed that it now was taking about an hour and a half to go through my list of roughly 500 items. Of course, I didn't have time to go through the list every day any more, but I religiously went through it at least once a week.

For some reason, I just didn't notice that the work was piling up. I was starting to miss deadlines for the first time in my life. I felt very stressed, but could not put my finger on why. I carried my OZ 9600 Model II everywhere, but I rarely opened it. I was just too busy.

Some part of my brain must have said enough because a strange thing started to happen. I started writing down short lists of things to do on scraps of paper and sticking them in my pocket. Whenever I thought of something urgent, I grabbed my paper and put it on the list. I took a highlighter and marked off what I had done during the day. At the end of the day, I dutifully put the items I did not complete in the OZ 9600 Model II, which now maintained more than 800 items.

Gradually, I forgot to enter those items in my organizer. I stopped using scraps of paper, and converted to a 5 x 8 sheet of paper that easily folded into my pocket. I never added more things than I could write on one side of the sheet. I transferred the incomplete items from the previous day's sheet only if I planned to do them that day. Otherwise the list item went in the trash.

I now spent five minutes a day preparing my list. The exercise of writing the list committed those daily items to memory, so even though I had the list in my pocket and read it only when I added or crossed off an item, I seldom forgot what was on it. I prioritized my tasks by what was most important, not by what I enjoyed doing, so I mentally reordered the list each time I added or deleted an item. As if by magic, my productivity returned. I blazed through the day, conquering tasks with ease. My stress diminished as my peace of mind improved. I finally realized how stupid I had been. The child of technology finally woke up.

And there you have it, my giant secret to success. A piece of paper and a pen.

I am certainly not the first one to come up with this. Dale Carnegie, one of my favorite authors, is a big proponent of the daily list. Unfortunately, he did not live long enough to experience the computer age and see how a computer can really mess up a perfectly good manual system.

If you discipline yourself to do nothing else, make sure you do a daily list. I notice that if I forget to make my list, even for one day, my productivity is instantly cut in half. Make a list. Do it by hand. Limit it to one side of one sheet. Write a new list every day. It's the cheapest, easiest secret weapon you'll ever find.

P.S. Here is a tip on how to prioritize. If you feel unsure about what to do first, do the thing that you dislike the most. I have found that ninety-five percent of the time what I dislike or dread doing is actually the thing that is most important and needs to be done first.

CHAPTER FORTY-NINE

DECIDE OR DON'T MEET

Who hasn't been in a meeting that dragged on forever, involved a dozen high paid people and accomplished absolutely nothing? When I was employed by a mega telephone company in my youth, I kept myself amused by calculating the joint salaries of those in attendance. I also, in my copious free time, calculated the cost of issuing a company letter. In 1980 dollars it was $242.50. It's no mystery to me why telephone bills are high!

Nothing strikes me as dumber than assembling a group of highly paid people to sit around, pontificate and do nothing. It is such a popular disease in American business that we should give it a name. I think it should be called the DUMM (Decidedly Useless Meaningless Monotonous) meeting syndrome.

In the U.S., logging time in these types of meetings is considered some sort of sick rite of passage. They only serve however, to salve the ego of the person by whose authority everyone was forced to come. The message is, "I am the big cheese. I can make you sit here and listen to endless people drone on and you cannot leave until I tell you it's okay." Doesn't this sound like a corporate "time out?"

At our company, meetings are not places to pontificate, they are places to evaluate differences of opinion and make decisions to act. The following is a list that contains guidelines to keep meetings short, productive, and fun.

1. Follow a written agenda. It will keep the group focused and can be used as an aid to get the group back on track if they go astray (and they will go astray!).

2. Add the phrase "Let's take that off line," to your repertoire, meaning: This item does not require discussion by the group at large, so discuss it privately with only those who need to participate and stop wasting everyone's time.

3. When a problem or question is posed, restate it for the group and solicit solutions. If additional information is required, get it immediately, if possible. Summon the missing individual, call somebody up and ask a question, excuse somebody from the meeting to go look something up or run a report. Aggressively get the information needed to make a decision RIGHT NOW.

4. Shut people down nicely when needed. "Paul, that's an interesting point, but I don't want to take the group's time to explore it right now. Let's move on so we can get everybody out of here and back to what they need to be doing."

5. Dismiss people who obviously don't need to be present. Once a meeting starts, it often becomes obvious that the presence of certain people is not required. Let them get back to their jobs.

6. Make fun (in a nice way) if people drone on. Fake snoring works well. The secret is to do it *consistently* to everyone. No one can be excluded. You even need to apply it to yourself when appropriate. (I generally feel someone has been effectively assimilated by the group when they snore as I drone on, or better yet, make fun of me when the opportunity presents itself.)

7. Sum up a topic of conversation with "Well, what do we want to do about this, _____?" Eyeball the person(s) in the group capable of making a decision on the subject, and supply their name in the sentence. Peer pressure alone will generally cause them to respond. If not, say "Do you think it would be a good idea to _____, what are your thoughts?" Just don't let

them off the hook with "I don't know," or "I'm not sure." Make them offer meaningful commentary.

8. After soliciting responses by those capable of offering a valid opinion, support one of the positions or your own position (which you should have expressed in turn) and give reasons for making your final decision.

9. Assign a time-line for execution of the decision by assigning a person to be responsible for completion of the task. Make sure everyone understands that the person responsible for seeing that the task gets done does not necessarily have to do the work. He only needs to make sure the work gets completed by the appropriate people within the time-line.

10. Estimate the anticipated length of the meeting and tell everyone at the start what that estimate is. If the meeting starts to bog down, simply say, "We need to pick up the pace. We are not on track to finish the meeting by the time we agreed. Let's whip through the remaining agenda items as quickly as possible." This never fails to give a meeting a second wind. It also focuses everyone on the time consumed so far and actually works to expedite the remainder of the meeting.

11. Don't be afraid to end on time and table remaining items. If you ran long because you spent time making final decisions in the meeting, this is a good thing. At least you won't have to revisit those topics. Enjoy your success on this front and simply schedule part two. It is a big mistake to let meetings routinely run over. Unbeknownst to you, the participants have full daily planners and the opportunity cost of messing up these schedules is something most entrepreneurs consistently fail to factor in. They feel their time is all-important, not realizing they may be costing the company many dollars by screwing up the schedules and possibly commitments of their reportees. DON'T fall into this trap. End on time.

Chapter Fifty

Insure Functions, Not People

Harry was indispensable. Every day when I drove into the parking lot, the first thing I did was to look for Harry's car.

Somehow we had muddled along before Harry, but frankly, I had forgotten how, as he now seemed to "take care of everything." I started worrying about how happy Harry was. I was concerned he might not be having a good time. Any time his office door was shut, I was sure he was talking to a headhunter. I started to smile more at Harry. I tried to do nice things for Harry. Harry quit.

There was no business reason why Harry quit, it was entirely personal as he had decided he wanted to live in a different part of the country. His announcement sent me into deep depression. I was sure we were doomed. The business would fail; we would never find another Harry. We had invested so much time in training him, and now we would have to start all over!

Did we get smarter? No! We hired Sam. We trained Sam. Sam became indispensable. Every day when I drove into the parking lot, the first thing I did was to look for Sam's car....

Sam, of course, ultimately quit. I was disillusioned. It was time to do some real entrepreneurial soul searching. What made Harry, then Sam indispensable? They certainly walked into the job knowing nothing.

It was the training we gave them collectively as a company that ultimately elevated them to a critical position.

Once they attained this position we began to feel the knowledge was all in their head. It wasn't. What we failed to realize was the knowledge came from and remained in the collective corporate head.

My favorite recurring characters from the Sci-Fi world of *Star Trek* are the Borg. Half human, half machine, these aliens are akin to super intelligent bees, living in a communal environment and possessing a collective mind that makes them an overwhelming power in the universe.

"Did we have a corporate collective like the Borg?" I thought. In fact, we did. Unfortunately, we could not plug ourselves into the wall Borg-style and get a brain transfer. Not only did we lack the nifty mechanical appendages, we also had the extra baggage of free will. How then, could the Borg help us?

One day we finally decided to "routinize." This is a cute little term often used by automation experts. It refers to reducing functions to their most elemental tasks and documenting the heck out of them so they can be done by a monkey (or Borg, as the case may be). We had learned the Borg secret. With tasks routinized, we now became interchangeable people as well. When someone was out ill, someone else merely opened the procedure book and followed the bouncing ball.

It's a little depressing when a TV show about space aliens is the source of your greatest managerial revelation! I guess I'll have to drop that famous mom expression, "There's nothing but junk on TV, why don't you read a book?" This is certainly a concession, but at least now I am far less concerned with where everyone has parked.

CHAPTER FIFTY-ONE

REVIEWS ARE BAD NEWS

The only thing that should be celebrated on an annual basis is a birthday.

Somehow a rumor got started in American business that every employee is entitled to an annual review. Perhaps it was started by Osama bin Laden or some other subversive force, for only someone who wished to scuttle the American economy would ever be a proponent of a system that yields nothing but dissatisfaction for everyone involved.

For many years I adhered to the annual review system. I dutifully filled out forms that referred to last year's goals and objectives. I circled little codes to rate employee performance as unacceptable or outstanding. Each review was a bloody battle masked only by a veil of corporate civility that kept both employer and employee from saying what they really wanted to say.

The message from each employee was consistent and clear. "I am clearly worth more than you are paying me. You need to recognize this and correct the situation. Further, I am worth more than my peers and I will start looking for a new job if you don't raise my salary by as much or more than others in my department. You get no credit for cost-of-living raises. I expect that. I will only acknowledge I got a raise if it exceeds a cost-of-living percentage."

My thoughts during the review were equally consistent. "This review process is a joke and a total waste of time. I am being forced to pay you for improved performance even if your contribution to the company has not improved. The only reason I am increasing your salary is to keep a lid on turnover because, if I don't, you will quit or you will whine incessantly, which will incite others to quit."

One day I just got fed up with the process and decided to stop reviewing. Instead of speaking with employees about their performance on an annual basis, I did it when I felt like it. I did it when I had something important to say. I didn't make a big deal out of it, I just casually asked the employee to come to my office and, starting on a positive note, told him how impressed I was with his actions or mentioned what a positive effect an act of his had had on the business. Typically the conversation evolved into a discussion of other subjects, and the two of us discussed, in a non-threatening manner, how he could best contribute to the company or what behavior of his was disruptive or unproductive and should be corrected. No money issues were discussed; no promises were made.

Adopting this method of review did not mean I abdicated my role as corporate disciplinarian. When a serious personnel issue arose, I dealt with it promptly and never combined it with a discussion of other topics. Instead, I focused on the issue at hand and put the employee on a program to correct the deficiency. Any termination that resulted was always swift, decisive, and well documented.

I soon discovered that abandoning the formal review process had no discernible impact on the setting of employee goals and objectives. In our company, objective setting had always been a continuing process, not an annual event. (If your company relies on annual reviews to set priorities and establish objectives you have far bigger problems than the personnel issues we are discussing here!)

Not only did review discussions become impromptu, but compensation discussions did as well, just for different reasons. Whether a raise could be given depended upon much more than whether an employee deserved it. It also depended upon the financial circumstances of the company and its ability to replace the individual at a like cost. I finally learned that raises depended upon a unique set of criteria and only one of these was the employee's level of contribution.

This revelation prompted me to sit down and reevaluate the open market value of each employee's position. I also evaluated the effectiveness of each individual in their particular job and adjusted this figure in light of individual accomplishment. Finally, I looked at each person's track record for trends, either good or bad, to decide whether an adjustment in salary to reinforce positive behavior was warranted. After this process was complete, I looked at both the current and projected company resources that could be earmarked for salary increases. The funds available were ultimately awarded to recipients by using every component in the evaluation process.

Raises were never given on a twelve-month anniversary and recipients never got a uniform percent. In fact, some people got multiple raises within a twelve-month period while others received nothing for three or more years. The time-line no longer mattered. Only true financial and performance measures went into the decision making process. Finally, we had dispelled the great American rumor.

And what was the result of this radical departure from tradition? It was incredible stability. No one pined away anymore over "review day." It became understood that the resources of the business, the talents of individuals and the availability of replacement talent were the sole factors controlling the process. The whining stopped. But more important, the quitting stopped. Turnover became almost non-existent.

The stars of the organization found themselves raised and promoted in step with their own progress and the company's financial growth. Those less motivated found themselves in a holding pattern but understood what it would take to earn more. By their actions, they made a conscious decision to insulate themselves from raises. Perhaps this is not what they wanted, but it is what they could easily predict, given their level of performance.

Life is far more pleasant for all concerned since we stopped performing routine reviews. Ironically, we now have more money to apportion to salary increases because less turnover has reduced our recruitment and training costs dramatically.

Don't be afraid to break with tradition. The best solution to your problem may be to start a tradition of your own.

CHAPTER FIFTY-TWO

CULTIVATE GRAPES

Sometimes, for a variety of reasons, you become attached to an employee throughout your career. As you change jobs, you arrange for her (or him) to follow. By default, she has an elevated stature over other employees because you have shared innumerable battles together. She understands how you think. You know how she will respond. She becomes your comfort food of business.

Janice was just such a person. As I moved from job to job, she came along. She knew me better than anyone with whom I had ever worked.

One summer morning, upon returning from a week's vacation, I was greeted by Janice, who wisely let me settle in and get my coffee before she approached. "We have a small problem," she told me, as she stared at her shoes. "We lost the entire database while you were gone. Nobody (meaning Janice) thought to back it up. We have to type everything in again. We've been typing for four days."

Only someone who knew me well would have realized the benefit of waiting an hour before springing this kind of news on me. From my adequately caffeinated vantage point, I responded calmly. "In light of the fact that you waited until I had my coffee, I will bypass my tirade on the subject and skip to the part where we figure out how to dig out of this hole."

Anyone else would have been reeling from a stinging reprimand or more likely, looking for a new job. My dependence on Janice however, had deadened my senses so I no longer evaluated Janice's sins objectively. Disciplinary acts never seemed to apply to Janice. She was a member of the inner circle and was immune from the standard rule set.

When I started my own company, I soon found a spot for Janice, making her manager of customer service. I was aware, from past relationships, that Janice could be a little rough around the edges, but her performance with clients encouraged me to ignore the intra-company spats that occasionally erupted around her. I needed her skill set and was glad I had convinced her to come.

One day our accounting manager came into my office and shut the door. "We have a problem," she said. "Carla is walking out." "Why?" I asked. "Because," continued Ellen, "Janice told her she was incompetent and hollered at her in front of a whole group of people. She fumbled a call that Janice said was important and Janice stormed up to her desk and just lit into her."

I sat stunned for a moment. Carla was our receptionist who had worked for the company less than three months. "I told Carla she should talk to you, but she's too scared." "Thank you for telling me," I said. "I've seen you solve problems like this before when you've had the chance," Ellen replied. "I think what happened was real unfair, and I wanted to make sure you knew what was going on before Carla walked out the door."

Ellen had worked for the company for five years. Time after time she had alerted me to circumstances, that because I was the boss, no one else would tell me about. By doing so, she gave me a chance to fix things, to reverse the tide in ugly situations and sometimes to intervene just before some personnel situation was about to blow. I thanked Ellen for once again aligning herself with me, the unapproachable owner. "Let me see what I can do," I said.

I called Janice into my office. "Janice," I said, "we have worked together and have been friends a long time. Today however, you crossed the line. You took advantage of your position and of your relationship with me and chewed up and spit out a defenseless person.

Carla is no match for you. You cannot attack a subordinate in front of her peers. I don't care what the offense was. You do not have the right to degrade someone and humiliate her to the point of tears. I'm afraid we are going to have to terminate our business relationship." Janice's jaw dropped visibly. "You're firing me?" she asked. "Yes I am," I answered.

It was a major wake up call for me as a manager. I had fraternized with an employee to such an extent that I had become blind to a management style I felt was abhorrent. I had played favorites. I finally realized what a big mistake I had made. I also learned something else. I woke up to the fact that my biggest unacknowledged ally had once again saved the day.

It was Ellen who needed to be recognized as the loyal one and an overwhelmingly important asset. She had consistently been the grape on the vine willing to give me information that I desperately needed to steer the company. Despite my misaligned allegiance to Janice, it was Ellen who deserved my respect and admiration.

When the word got out that I had fired my long-time comrade Janice, who made more than three times what Carla made, the company reeled from the shock. The shock though, was overwhelmingly good. It spawned the feeling that justice was still alive and well in the corporate world.

Carla stayed on and we soon recovered from Janice's departure. That day, many people reevaluated their opinion of me and of the company. The "justice" behind the decision to fire the powerful and retain the meek brought solidarity to the company and gave me a much-improved rapport with many of the employees.

I vowed never to do such a stupid thing again. I would not ignore obvious signposts because of a personal history with someone. More importantly, I would recognize loyalty to the company and to myself personally, and I would make a point to cultivate those people who displayed their allegiance.

An important corner had been turned in the business. And whom did I have to thank for my personal wake up call? Ellen. Ellen, who took the risk to champion the cause of an oppressed coworker, despite my strong allegiance to her foe. Ellen, who had nothing personally to gain from seeing Carla retained. Ellen, who had no special tie to either the company or me. Why then, did she do it? She did it because it was the right thing to do.

I hadn't recognized Ellen's wonderful contributions in the past, but I was not going to make the same mistake in the future. I immediately took steps to make sure Ellen understood she had done a great thing and that I appreciated her decision to display her loyalty and trust by informing me about a situation I really needed to know about.

When the unexpected happens, there are no better safety nets than the ones built by those who will clue you in to the inner workings of the company.

Just make sure the corporate grapes you cultivate are the ones with heart, not the ones who have your number.

CHAPTER FIFTY-THREE

WHAT SEPARATES THE MEN FROM THE BOYS? THEIR NOTES

Everyone is sitting around the conference table. Critical information that everyone will need to recall is being delivered by the speaker. My gaze takes in everyone around the room. There are no pens moving.

Note taking is apparently considered to be as useful as knowing a dead language. It's right up there with Latin. But what will everyone do when they have to recall what is being said? They will try to wing it. Later, when things are not proceeding well because no one has any notes to go by, I will charge in and, as leader of the pack, use my notes to get everyone back on track.

I have been known to say in meetings, "Pick up your pen *now* and start writing." Invariably, pens are picked up but they do not touch the paper. Apparently holding the pen in the correct writing position is considered enough to humor "Mom."

I have preached, ordered, begged and distributed my guide to successful note taking, yet my employees still do not write anything down. If nothing else, my employees should take notes just to suck up to me, to insure future raises and promotions.

Why then, do I include a chapter on note taking in this book? Because you are the entrepreneur who will be far more successful if you master this skill. You are reading this book hopefully to learn some helpful tricks of the trade. I am including this chapter because I want *someone* to actually benefit from a really great tool that I have perfected over the years and from which I have benefited greatly. I have given up on my employees, but I have not given up on you!

We all allegedly learned to take notes in school. Most of us however, were more than happy to leave note taking behind when we graduated. This is unfortunate, because one of the biggest weapons in business is the ability to drive projects through to completion. This is pretty hard to do if you can't remember what it is that you are trying to drive.

Most projects in business die from benevolent neglect. Employees do not refuse to do things, they *forget* to do them. As a manager, I spend a significant part of my day running around reminding people to do what they have agreed to do because they have forgotten. I e-mail them, buzz them on the phone, remind them in meetings, and leave stickies on their desks. And why is all this necessary? Because they refuse to take notes. After all, note taking is what they had to do in high school and they are grown up now. They say they can remember. They say they are beyond taking notes. Oh yeah? Au contraire. At a minimum, big ego.

Unless you possess a photographic memory, there is no way you can retain all the information given in a meeting. In most cases, you will not even be able to remember the gist of the meeting two weeks later.

For three years I went to law school. Since I never practiced law, most people wonder why I subjected myself to such torture. I believe it was one of the best things I ever did for several reasons. First, I became convinced I never wanted to marry an attorney. Next, I learned to write a pretty mean contract, which has saved the company a lot of money and kept us out of legal hot water for many years. Finally, and most important, I learned how to take notes that capture the moment, record significant details, and preserve the information "gems" of every meeting.

Most law school students quickly understand that you either take notes or die. Law professors don't slow down or repeat because you didn't get it the first time. It is survival of the fastest pen that rules.

From this painful experience I have compiled a short and to the point guide detailing how to take notes effectively.

If you will merely follow the note taking methods outlined below, you will find that others in the company will naturally follow your lead when they discover you are the only one well documented enough to clearly point the way. It is the best way I know to add to your power as an entrepreneur or manager.

KEYS TO SUCCESSFUL NOTE TAKING

ALWAYS USE 8.5 X 11 INCH PAPER

- Full-page notes can be photocopied and filed easily.

- Notebooks can be used to organize notes, if required.

- Full-page notes are not as likely to get lost—never use small pads or stickies.

- Larger paper encourages you to use complete sentences.

ALWAYS DATE EACH PAGE AND INCLUDE THE YEAR

- Dating allows a time-line to be determined when facts change in subsequent meetings.

- It is very important to have dates if notes become part of a legal proceeding.

- Dates allow time intervals between requests and fulfillment of requests to be determined.

- Time frames are needed by others who may ultimately receive a copy of your notes.

ALWAYS NOTE ALL ATTENDEES OF A MEETING AND INDICATE WHO SAID WHAT DURING THE MEETING

- No one's memory is that good.

- What you are sure you can remember typically remains accurate less than twenty-four hours.

- It is *very* important in legal proceedings to be able to link comments to an individual.

- Linking people with their titles or functional positions is important for future reference.

- It helps you transfer name/phone/e-mail information obtained during the meeting, to your address book.

WRITE DOWN EVERYTHING

- Think of yourself as a stenographer. Do not decide on the fly what is important.

- Write enough notes to be able to reconstruct the whole meeting for someone who didn't attend.

- Only abbreviate standard words like "w/" for with or "&" for and. Recipients of your notes will find them worthless if you use personal abbreviations.

NEVER ASSUME SOMEONE ELSE WILL TAKE ADEQUATE NOTES FOR YOU

- Your perspective as to what is important will always be different from someone else's.

- You are dependent upon someone else's note taking skills.

- Taking notes in your own words substantially improves your recall.

- Copies of notes are never a good substitute for the original.

NEVER CO-MINGLE NOTES FROM TWO DIFFERENT MEETINGS ON ONE PAGE

- It makes it impossible to file notes without copying them first.

- Co-mingled notes often confuse even the author.

- Notes cannot be distributed to others without cutting and pasting.

WRITE LEGIBLY AND LOGICALLY ENOUGH THAT SOMEONE ELSE CAN READ YOUR NOTES WITHOUT HELP

- Many people find it difficult to read their own hastily written notes weeks or months later.

- Why struggle when a little neatness goes a long way?

- What is clear on an original often becomes unreadable on a photocopy.

USE A DARK PEN

- Pen cannot be erased so it stands up far better in a legal proceeding.

- Photocopies are cleaner and easier to read.

- Penned notes do not get smudged when you stick them in a file.

- Note taking with a pen is faster than note taking with a pencil.

REVIEW YOUR NOTES AT THE END OF THE MEETING

- Immediate review allows you to ask other attendees to fill in any gaps you have in your own notes.

- Reviewing notes while they are still fresh lets you identify the most important meeting points so they can be emphasized or highlighted for future reference.

- If something that you wrote doesn't make sense, you can clear it up by comparing notes with others.

LEARN TO LEAVE SENTENCES HALF FINISHED IF THE MEETING'S PACE IS TOO QUICK TO ALLOW YOU TO WRITE EVERYTHING

- Each time there is a lull, quickly go back and finish any undone sentences.

- Do not sacrifice neatness in order to keep up with the speaker.

- Use the buddy system and arrange to get missing pieces from another participant.

- Photocopy other people's notes to fill in the gaps.

MAKE A TO DO LIST FROM YOUR NOTES BEFORE FILING

- It's almost guaranteed that action items will be scattered throughout your notes.

- Twenty-four hours later you won't remember TO DO items from the notes any better than the notes themselves.

ALWAYS FILE YOUR NOTES

- Don't bother to recopy or type notes. Your memory of events will be better, looking at the original.

- Always distribute notes before you file them, otherwise they will never get distributed.

- Make sure your pages are numbered 1 of 1 etc. This is important legally to show completeness.

IF YOU ARE IN CHARGE OF THE MEETING, USE YOUR NOTES TO ASSIGN TASKS BEFORE ADJOURNING

- It makes it unnecessary to have a second meeting to assign tasks later.

- Assigning tasks immediately insures that projects are started as soon as possible.

- Immediate assignment helps insure that no task goes unassigned or is inadvertently assigned to two people.

CHAPTER FIFTY-FOUR

THE POWER OF THE PEN

In grammar school we all allegedly learned to write. Some spinster somewhere with an anorexic posture and an attitude to go with it, made us learn the difference between active and passive voice and the admirable qualities of the semicolon. What a relief when spell check and grammar check arrived on the scene. They freed us from revisiting the unpleasant memories of our youth.

I don't think so! If good business writing only depended upon spelling and grammar, we would be home free. But alas, the power behind the written word frequently eludes the entrepreneur, for good writing is all a matter of tone.

Sometimes in business, you inherit a customer. This happens most often when the company with whom you do business sells out (occasionally to some very unsavory characters.) In 1992 this is exactly what happened to one of our major accounts. When I first met the new "boys in charge," I knew we were in trouble. Oil always floats to the top and the slick created by these boys could be seen for miles. To them, I was merely a little naive businesswomen they could steam roll. Their tone was insulting; their demands were endless. They were cell phone toting, power lunching egomaniacs who were clearly not above sawing off the legs of their guest chairs to make themselves feel bigger.

It quickly became apparent that the object of their game was to abscond with the billing database in direct violation of their contract, convert their billing to another system they had pilfered from a third party and then suddenly pull the plug on us. They apparently believed that by doing this, we would be left with no way to collect the many thousands of dollars they would then owe.

Did I get out my Marlin, my Winchester or my Luger? No, I had a far better weapon. I got out my Cross. Each week, I wielded my pen and responded to what they thought were subtle requests to steal a portion of the database. I gave them enough of what they wanted to allay their suspicions, while I systematically built an audit trail worthy of Price Waterhouse. I also required them to pay as they went, crying that we were just a little company and couldn't possibly afford to keep processing without some cash from their big strong company. Aren't inflated entrepreneurial egos wonderful?

When they finally did pull the plug, I messengered over our documentation to our attorney. I could hear him smiling over the phone. "This stuff nails them to the wall," he said. "I know. Let's get'em," I answered. Our attorney packaged our case with great finesse. Discovery ensued. We found out during the depositions, that the new owners had criminal records. Big surprise! At the end of our legal road, the judge awarded us over $150,000 and court costs. I smiled as I put my Cross back in its holster, ready for the next time it might be needed to defend the realm.

I credit the success of this skirmish and many other business battles to the effective use of tone. For it is tone (the feeling generated by what we write) that drives the reader to the proper emotional destination. Over the years I have used my ability to write like a sword. I have defended the business, attacked unruly business partners, managed difficult clients, and kept employees disciplined and productive.

Because I consider writing to be one of the ultimate tools of business, I have tried to improve the writing skills of numerous employees. What I have discovered is that grammar and punctuation can readily be taught. What eludes most people is the construction of a letter that conveys the right tone. With the proper tone, we can drive the reader wherever we want him to go.

The process of writing must always begin by identifying a purpose. Just ask yourself, what am I trying to achieve? What action am I trying to trigger; what emotion am I trying to elicit or quell?

I never worry about the details of my writing until I have a handle on the proper tone. Do I want to sound mad and ready to rip somebody's heart out? Am I trying to be conciliatory or condescending? Hostile or intimidating? Threatening or apologetic?

After turning on spell check and perhaps grammar check you are now armed to do warfare with a pen. My advice is to begin by writing a stream of consciousness letter. Let the words flow just as you would talk. Don't stop to fix spelling or grammar. Do not worry about sentences that are too long. The goal is merely to capture the desired tone on paper. If you fool around with corrections, you will lose your momentum and what you write will be ineffective.

Now take the tone test yourself. Read it back and see what you've got. If it was truly stream of consciousness writing, going back and rereading feels like you are reading someone else's writing. What is on the page is often a surprise. Now ask, "How does it hit me? What emotions does it stir in me? Am I feeling charitable towards the author or irritated? Is my inclination to throw the letter in the trash? Is the letter able to capture my attention sufficiently to cause me to want to finish reading it?"

Next, put it aside to allow time for your emotional stance to change. If you still feel the same way upon a second review, your tone is at least consistent with a static emotional state. If not, try again. Rewrite is a seven-letter, not a four-letter word. Just accept the human side of your nature, and when necessary, edit what you wrote, at least until the profanity and animal descriptions have been removed.

Sometimes after writing a letter, I notice the message conveyed is clearly, "stick it up your butt and twirl." Perhaps at the moment the letter was drafted, that was indeed what I wished to convey. Sometimes however, after some time has elapsed, I decide that the original tone no longer seems proper. Perhaps I now feel I would like to modify the tone to convey, "stick it up your butt and twirl *slowly*." It is review of tone, after time has elapsed, that helps insure that the proper tone is ultimately conveyed.

Once you have tone under control, it's time to apply *The Elements of Style*, by William Strunk, Jr. It is the finest book ever written for making the written word the powerful tool it can be. And amusingly enough, it's a little skinny book. If you are serious about becoming a writer capable of keeping a hostile client at bay, attracting sales prospects, handling a difficult bank, or keeping the lid on a litany of personnel issues, READ STRUNK. It is invaluable *and* quick! For those who prefer their grammatical lessons to be packaged with a little humor, I suggest reading *Woe Is I*, by Patricia T. O'Conner. I think Strunk would approve.

After adjusting tone, it is time to find someone whose judgment you respect to read the letter. Just because you think that it hits the mark doesn't mean your audience does.

My father fulfilled the role of reviewer and advisor for me for many years. Not only did he shorten (rip and slash) my correspondence, he also supplied an objective opinion on the true tone of what I had written. This is where years of living serves as a good litmus test to determine if your writing hits the mark. Look for someone with appropriate experience who is older and wiser. Many neophytes have learned to look brilliant by asking and then acting upon the advice of others.

Ask your advisor to read what you have written and see what tone he or she feels is being conveyed. You are striving for a consensus between yourself and your advisor. At least if you and your advisor agree, there will be two people in the world who take what you wrote the same way. If you pick somebody who is as off the wall as yourself, well... let's just say you are better off going with someone who "complements" your unique personality.

Now do the step that nearly everyone skips. Read the finished product over several times. I have lost count of how many times the mistake I ultimately found was discovered on the third or fourth read. Because you are familiar with what you wrote, you tend to skim, not read. Read carefully. One typo can negate every bit of benefit a powerful and purposeful tone can create. Don't blow it. Make sure it is error-free.

In eighteen years, my company has never been sued. I attribute this largely to my writing skills. Ambiguities with clients have been cleared up and documented through carefully written letters. Vendors have been forced to perform in part, because of letters that clearly spelled out the consequences of their failure to live up to their contractual obligations. Those failing to pay have been effectively reminded of their financial obligations. Collectors seeking payment have been placed at ease by carefully worded promises to pay that left adequate wiggle room.

Writing well is coercion with a pen. It is powerful. It is effective. It is a tool that costs very little to use; yet as a business skill, it has atrophied in many entrepreneurs. Writing is the one competitive edge that once mastered, remains yours for life and can never be taken away. How can a business tool get any better than that?

Here is a recap of the steps to good writing.

1. Decide what you are trying to achieve and the tone you will need to do it.

2. Do "stream of consciousness" writing to achieve the desired tone.

3. Revisit what you have written and objectively evaluate tone.

4. Tweak tone as necessary.

5. Apply *Strunk* to what you have written.

6. Solicit the opinion of an advisor and fix as necessary.

7. Reread at least three times looking for tone, spelling, and grammar problems.

A STRESS-FREE LIFE
IN A
STRESS-FILLED WORLD

CHAPTER FIFTY-FIVE

EVERYONE CAN QUIT BUT YOU

Sad but true, everyone can quit but you!

There are times in your life when you just want to bail. You're tired, frustrated, scared, overwhelmed, overloaded, and discouraged. You are surrounded by enemies on all sides, and everyone wants a chunk of you.

Employees pop into your office explaining they only need "a minute" of your time. Clients chide you for not getting back to them quickly enough. Spouses remind you of missed family obligations. Children compare you to moms who don't work. Spouses and particularly children feel that if you are home, you belong to them. "Excuse me," says the beleaguered entrepreneur, "I don't agree. Somewhere in there, there needs to be time for me!"

If you can't quit, what can you do? You can cope. I have, by no means, reached some Mecca of inner peace, but I have learned how to carry the world on my shoulders without turning to Valium, Prozac, alcohol, or worse yet, becoming a Looney Tune. I do it with my arsenal of coping tools.

THE ARSENAL

GET ENOUGH SLEEP

This one is as old as the hills and is probably the single most critical tool in coping with overload. You must be fueled for battle. What goes in the engine? Food and sleep do, and sleep heads the list as most important. I need at least seven and a half hours which I have always found to be terribly inconvenient. Maybe my need for this much sleep is God's not so subtle way of telling me to slow down. "What part of ENOUGH don't you understand?" says God. "All of it," I reply. "Gotcha," says God.

DEMAND TIME FOR YOURSELF

Do not let your family and your business usurp all your time. This does not mean you must sacrifice family time. There are other ways to cope at a price that is far less costly. Stop obligatory entertaining. Do not just sit in the same room with your family, zone out, and watch TV. Stop looking at all the junk that comes in the mail. Fight for these time slots. They can all be reclaimed as chunks of personal time.

Once you have preserved a small chunk of time, make the most of it. Each of us has a list of things we like to do in our down-time. It's not necessary to do all of these things each week, just make sure that a week never goes by that does not include at least a couple of down-time items. My list consists of painting, reading, watching old movies, roller blading, horseback riding, playing my guitar, shopping for fun stuff like art supplies or things for my horse, and working on my latest business brainstorm.

I have tried to make clear to my family that I am not to be interrupted when I am involved in one of these activities. When my family fails to take my need for down-time seriously, occasionally I am forced to push back and make it known that I will not tolerate their usurpation of my precious down-time when they feel the need to interrupt. Sometimes I do this subtly by asking, "Is the house, on fire?" when they knock on my office door.

LEARN TO PURGE

When you are at the top, there is no one who is totally safe to dump on. The only safe way involves a piece of paper and a pen. It's not automated or computerized and does not require the services of a counselor. Just put the pen to paper and let it go. Write until the pen slows down. Get it all out. Write about anything you want.

When you write you don't have to be kind, fair or unprejudiced. You don't have to be a good mother or fight fair with your spouse. Just get it out, so those feelings can die a natural death, letting you move on to stiller and more productive waters. I have been writing for thirty years. I only do so occasionally these days, but when it's time, it's time. Start by writing on a regular schedule. You will soon find out how often and how much you need to write based on the relief writing brings.

DO NOT ACT YOUR AGE

Do not act your age. My daughter is fond of saying "You still act like a kid, Mom. I think that is so cool." I have not abdicated my job as mom; I just still remember how to have fun. I try never to think of myself as too old to do something. I don't mind being the oldest roller blader in the neighborhood. I like acting goofy with my daughter. If I do face painting on my daughter, I let her do my face too. Why not? There is enough garbage in life. And I really, *really* mean it when I say I couldn't care less what people think of me. I have better things to do than to let others dictate my sense of self-worth.

LIVE IN DAY-TIGHT COMPARTMENTS

This really great tool comes from Dale Carnegie, an icon among authors of business advice. In one of his books he describes how, on a big ship, certain sections can be cordoned off in case a leak occurs to prevent the entire ship from flooding. He makes an analogy from these water-tight compartments to day-tight compartments by which a person can cordon off the past and the future and thereby isolate the present.

We must do so, he believes, because worrying about what has happened or might happen only causes stress and frustration. We can only affect change in the here and now. This simple analogy has helped me over hundreds of rough spots by simply returning my focus to where it ought to be in the first place.

LEAN ON OTHERS; GET AN OUTSIDE ADVISOR

My father was my sage advisor for many years. Frequently his response to a question I asked was "You dumb bunny, blah, blah, blah, that's why you should listen to your old man." His "dumb bunny" comments were his way of pointing out (not too subtly) that I was simply too close to the situation to look at it objectively. I credit him with the survival (and once the virtual resurrection) of the business, as he objectively sized up situations with brutal honesty and offered advice on both personal and business problems. Coping with the responsibility of decision making is far easier when some of that load can be placed on another set of broad, competent shoulders, particularly when that individual is not affected by the outcome of the decision.

When he died, I lost not just a father and a friend, but a sounding board and an advisor. Not only did I reel from the loss, but the business did too. Things at work and at home sagged as subjective decision making prevailed. I finally realized that while no one could replace Dad, at least his role as business advisor could be performed by someone else.

When we found Mike, a professional business advisor, I rediscovered how wonderful the addition of outside perspective could be. It improved decision-making by adding critical objectivity. Not only did the business benefit from outside advice, I also benefited from the calming influence it provided to me personally. I no longer felt all alone in a rowboat drifting in the high seas of business. At least I felt that I was in radio contact with the Coast Guard and they had a couple of suggestions on how to get back to shore if I cared to listen.

Mike is not the panacea of advice that Dad was, but he is experienced, thoughtful and as interested in the success of the business as any outsider can be. I cannot stress enough how important obtaining an objective outside advisor can be. If you can find someone to advise you personally as well as professionally, so much the better.

TAKE THE EMOTION OUT OF DECISION MAKING

Emotion creeps into decision making most often when it is difficult to identify the importance of pros and cons surrounding a decision. By adopting a simple method to evaluate these pros and cons objectively, many problems virtually solve themselves. The following method works as well for deciding whether you should extend your daughter's curfew as it does for whether you should move your business to a new location.

Just take out a piece of paper. Draw a line down the center of it and write "FOR" and "AGAINST" at the top of the page. Write down the pros and cons in the appropriate column. Now here's the trick. Assign a weighted number to each pro and con using a scale from one to three to indicate the point's importance. Add up the weighted values for each one and see which column wins. It's quick, easy, and amazingly accurate. Most important, it helps you reach a decision that is final. It typically removes the desire to revisit decisions because all pros and cons *and* their relative importance have been factored in.

Here is a recap of the arsenal:

1. Get enough sleep.

2. Demand (and get) down-time for yourself.

3. Learn to purge—get it all out on paper.

4. Do not act your age.

5. Live in "day-tight" compartments.

6. Get yourself a sage advisor.

7. Adopt a weighted pro and con method for decision making.

You may not be able to quit if you're the boss, but coping well can be the next best thing. In fact, it may ultimately be better. Few entrepreneurs

I know would relish the idea of once again, letting someone else tell them what to do. I think the goal is generally to get through it, not get out of it. With the proper arsenal you can do just that.

Chapter Fifty-Six

Margin, More Than A Term For Stock Brokers

There is a certain part of every entrepreneur that feels invincible. We sincerely believe we can do it all. Our breed blends ego and childish curiosity to foster a unique kind of bravery suitable for starting a business. Many of us still believe in Santa.

It is this brash, youthful outlook on life that makes us over-achievers. The flip side is that we are typically over-doers as well.

When my little girl was four, we decided we would take a Mommy/Katie trip up to our cabin in New York State. The night before, I packed our bags. Dismayed, I looked at the pile of luggage. Packing light was a foreign concept to me. It was something that tourists in Europe do who are willing to wash out their underwear every night and turn a polyester pant suit inside out to create a minimum of fourteen separate outfits. I made peace with the luggage mountain. I wanted the luxury of a flannel bathrobe and newly laundered underwear every day.

Six bags graced the front hall. I looked at my daughter hopefully. "Do you think you can carry your own bag Katie?" I flexed my arm muscles hoping to inspire her to say yes. "Sure I can, Mommy!" and she tugged her wheelie suitcase, halting and jerking down the hall.

We left for the airport an hour and twenty minutes before the flight was scheduled to leave. I knew it took forty-five minutes to get to the airport, but I had to squeeze in one last call to the office, make the two of us snacks for the airplane, and check Katie's bag to make sure she had packed all the stuffed animals needed to keep her world secure.

As we entered the acceleration ramp to the highway, a tidal wave of stress began to surge. There was no acceleration in "acceleration ramp." It was rush hour. Two million Denverites were on their way to work. Most of them were idling just ahead of us, drinking coffee.

When we reached the airport, the short-term parking lot was full. I looked out on a sea of unnumbered rows in remote. I looked at Katie and patted her knee. We'll find a spot," I told her, "but were going to have to hurry." "Mommy, the veins in your head are sticking out!" "Mommy is just excited about our trip," I answered, as I swung into a parking space nine nautical miles from the terminal.

I loaded up the wheelie and handed Katie her suitcase. "Run!" I yelled, as I frantically tugged at the load behind me. I suddenly had a much better understanding of inertia. In the terminal, I noticed Katie's face was flushed as I tried to encourage her to hurry. "See if you can beat me to the door," I gasped. "I'm too tired Mommy, I want to stop." I looked at my watch. I became desperate. "We can't stop, Katie. You need to run faster!" A man looked at me, convinced I was breaking some kind of child labor law.

The gate was just ahead. I could feel the scene becoming a slow motion movie clip, as we dove for the podium. The ticket agent looked at me serenely. "You're too late," she said. "No, I'm not," I answered. "The plane is sitting right there." "The door is shut," she stated, without moving her lips. "Then open the door. I don't see the problem," I said in winded gasps. She looked through me, unseeing, as if she had the authority, as Queen of Ticketing, to banish me from the terminal. "Please, *please* let us on the plane," I begged. Could this be happening? (Not the missing the plane part, but the begging part.) "No. The next plane is in three hours," Her Majesty answered.

"We missed the plane," I told Katie. She began to cry. "We have time to go to McDonald's and have breakfast." "Yeah!" said Katie. I smiled and wished an Egg McMuffin could have the same effect on me.

As we sat in McDonald's, I felt defeated. Somehow I had always been able to pull things out. What had happened? I felt as if my blueprint for life no longer worked. It should have been no big deal to take another flight, but it *was* a big deal. It made me question how I did everything in my life. I was always cutting things too thin. I never left enough time to do anything. There was never any margin for error.

I knew margin was the operative word. Whether it was catching a plane, making an appointment, or planning a new product offering, I never left any time for unexpected events. I always lived on the edge in order to cram in as much of life as I possibly could. And what was the price I paid to do this? It was immense stress. Continual, unrelenting stress that eroded the very thing I was trying to improve, the quality of life. Somehow I thought if I achieved more, I would somehow be a better and more satisfied person.

I have tried to learn from this lesson by working to identify situations where allowing margin for error is imperative. I did this by taking a piece of paper and listing obligations that most often generated stress when I failed to meet them. I ranked the list and then used it to determine when it was really important to me to add margin.

I still live on the edge. Lifetime habits are hard to break. I have however, made some improvements, and I have learned to add margin to the equation when the stress stakes are extremely high. I don't think I will ever miss another plane.

Provided below is the list I used to rank my own stress generators. I suggest that you add and delete items in order to customize the list for yourself, and then try to rank the items according to the stress they generate in you. If you can consciously add margin to the top few items, I believe you will feel, as I do, that adding margin is often truly the best way to over-achieve.

STRESS GENERATORS

1. Being a little late (under 15 minutes).

2. Being a lot late (over 15 minutes).

3. Missing appointments completely.

4. Missing your children's activities.

5. Missing your spouse's activities.

6. Missing client deadlines.

7. Firing employees.

8. Taking collection calls.

9. Pleading with the bank to extend your credit.

10. Missing your stress-buster activities.

11. Missing financial obligations.

12. Admitting to outsiders that your business has problems.

CHAPTER FIFTY-SEVEN

FIND YOUR MAGIC HOUR AND FIGHT FOR IT

I am not a morning person. I am not a night person. I guess midday works for me. At least I used to think so. Then, about twelve years ago, tragedy struck me personally. My infant daughter died.

I was inconsolable and the deep sighs I expelled hour after hour were my body's feeble attempt to purge the pain. The pain was deep and sorrowful. Like waves of silent moaning, it ebbed and flowed, an ocean of loss. It was silent suffering that time did nothing to heal. I no longer could sleep. I only functioned well when whatever was competing for my conscious thought edged out everything else.

The worst time of day was 4:00 a.m., the hour we lost Betsy. Every night I awoke just before that hour and stayed awake until exhaustion made sleep inevitable. Eventually I started getting up at that hour. The house was quiet and I searched for things to focus on, not to escape the memories but to momentarily distract myself from them. I learned that you never escape the pain of loss; you only learn to incorporate it into your consciousness where it safely waits to be revisited.

I listened to books on tape. I read books capable of adequately capturing my attention. The years passed and I grew to love this hour of solitude. Most nights I would return to bed for a final hour of sleep when the reading, reflection, and study sufficiently quieted the anxiety that raged away within me.

With time, the pain became an old friend, and I accepted my nocturnal respite as something that was nurturing and good for my mental health. I came to look forward to that time and realized my mind was sharpest then. I did my best thinking then, unfettered by interruptions, demands made by others, or the pangs of conscience to be doing something "off the list."

I now devote my hour to reading something new I want to learn. I feel driven to read things that teach me rather than things that entertain me. Early in the morning is "my time." I guard it zealously. It helps me grow. It helps me stay grounded. It's my key to mental health.

I have known others who have carved out a small portion of the day for quiet soul repairing and feel it is the most important thing they do for themselves. I include myself in this group. My family knows not to disturb me during that hour unless the house is on fire. I have actually posted a sign to that effect on my home office door, lest anyone should forget.

My hour has allowed me to learn things and grow personally for many years. It is amazing what can be accomplished in a single hour of uninterrupted time. I am not necessarily advocating 4:00 a.m. Different strokes for different folks. Just find your time and zealously guard it.

We all need the peace of mind that solitude brings. I only regret what caused me to understand this. Reality may be a cruel teacher, but she is also a good teacher. What a crime it would be to go through the pain but ignore the lesson.

CHAPTER FIFTY-EIGHT

NEVER GIVE OUT YOUR HOME PHONE

One peaceful evening at home, the phone rang. It was a client. It was at least five minutes before I could get a word in edgewise. And what was the reason for all this blustering? He had a problem with his billing. Could I confirm that the problem was legitimate from home? No. Could I do anything to correct the situation if it was? No. Did the phone call take me away from my family, our shared dinner hour, my favorite TV show, and interfere with my "decompression" time? Absolutely.

Nothing good happens when you let work infiltrate your home life. It is like an insidious disease. At first, there are only minor interruptions. So what if your child was in the middle of telling you his accomplishments for the day? The interruption only takes a minute. After all, the kids are old enough to put themselves to bed. They will understand if Mommy has to be on the phone with the office occasionally.

And who says you can't take it with you? Think how much more productive you will be by taking care of matters as they come up so that you won't have to leave them looming until the next day. Isn't that why we have pagers and cell phones?

Twenty years from now, when time with my daughter has been reduced to Christmas get-togethers and the occasional holiday or birthday celebration, I will thank God I did not cave every time a client or business associate asked for my home phone number. For many years I have zealously protected my private life. To me, it is no different than a celebrity fighting to preserve his or her private existence. We all want, need, and deserve a life unconnected with our vocation. As the pace of life has sped up, many people have lost sight of this line of demarcation, and they have the stress and neuroses to prove it.

When a business associate asks for my home number, I always tell him, "The best way to reach me is by e-mail. I check it frequently and e-mail allows me to forward any question or concern you have to the proper person immediately." I follow this with a quick change to a benign subject, having once again successfully defended my personal realm.

I also do not carry a cell phone unless I am traveling on business. The cell phone I do use is installed in my car. I find there is no opportunity cost to being on the phone while driving other than the occasional near miss that occurs when I fail to multi-task adequately. I find judicious use of driving time further protects family time by expanding my workday.

I realize that the clients I have declined to give my home phone number to may feel some irritation over my unwillingness to remain at their beck and call. So be it.

Being able to sit quietly with my daughter while she tells me her secrets or shares her problems makes me forget I even have clients and leaves me with memories I will cherish long after the business has been forgotten.

CHAPTER FIFTY-NINE

GIVE YOUR BABY A JOB

In 1991 I had a baby. It was a welcome event but I was not sure how to integrate this new being into my ten hour a day work schedule. Consistent with my type A personality, I was back in the office three days after giving birth with my daughter peacefully napping in the corner of my office. Did I say peacefully? That lasted about twenty minutes. As she screamed at the top of her lungs, the waves of panic moved in. Even as queen of multitaskers, I could not multitask this! My solution was this ad:

> Wanted: Nanny to care for newborn in office setting for business owner. Will train in office administration duties. Office functions to be performed as time permits. No office experience necessary. Great career opportunity!

The Nanny we hired was fabulous. Trish remained an employee for over three years and did data entry and filing during "nap time." It was a very harmonious relationship. Trish and Katie shared an oversized office equipped with a desk, computer, playpen, crib, toy bin, art board, changing table, telephone and filing cabinets.

Not only did Katie have an office, she had a title. We put her on the organizational chart as Director of Morale.

Each day at lunch I would get Katie, and we would take walks around the neighborhood. We went to the library at the end of the street or to Woolworths to eat lunch at the counter. We visited the guys at the fire station or sat on the front steps of the building and ate our sack lunches. I have wonderful memories of those times because the stress of the outside world disappeared when we were together.

Whenever I was having a particularly hard day, I would go downstairs and take a "Katie break." I found that other employees occasionally took Katie breaks for therapeutic reasons as well, and that her presence was positive for the company overall. It's nice to visit someone whose biggest problem is finding the right crayon!

Katie also learned some basic office skills while being employed as Director of Morale. One day, when Katie was two and a half, she heard the phone ringing at the front desk as she walked by. Katie stopped and picked up the phone. "Hello," she said. "Take a message please."

As a business owner you can employ someone to watch your own child without needing to qualify as a day care center. Be sure to take advantage of this special perk which is easy to defend to your staff, since it cannot be offered to others unless the company becomes a licensed day care facility. Not only will it distress you, it just might brighten the day of others in the office as well.

Chapter Sixty

Outsource Your Stress; Get A Horse

In my youth I owned a horse. It was a wonderful diversion and kept to a minimum my involvement in things that all parents fear. With that chapter of my life closed, I pursued more adult activities, while my horse paraphernalia collected dust in the basement.

Remembering the fond memories of youth, as did my husband Rick, whose experiences paralleled my own, we purchased a pony for our nine-year-old daughter, Katie.

For those who have never owned a horse, it is a way of life, not simply an acquisition. You get sucked into a philosophy that requires you to leave behind petty, selfish, and materialistic goals in favor of building a relationship with an animal and putting something first beside yourself. For Katie, the magic began, and her proud parents watched the transformation. What we didn't notice was the transformation within ourselves. For the first time in years, we began placing something above business in our personal priority systems.

One day, Katie's trainer brought a bedraggled and seriously underfed horse back to the stable. She had attended an auction where she had witnessed bidding on a horse that appeared to have little to recommend her. Helen, having been around horses all her life, sensed something in this mare worth saving. Since only the "killers" were bidding on the horse, she felt a pull to save the horse's life. That night she brought Lacey back to the stable.

Lacey's conformation was poor and she was seriously underweight. Helen told us she would use her to give riding lessons. After Lacey had recovered somewhat, Helen attempted to do just that, but Lacey's past was too checkered for her to be the calm personality needed for schooling children. "What are you going to do with her?" I asked Helen. "I don't know," she said. "She's just too difficult for children to ride."

One thing common to all entrepreneurs is their inability to resist a challenge. I retained a dim recollection of a girl, who at sixteen, could ride bareback and handle difficult horses with ease. Did that girl still exist in the now forty-five-year-old body? "Helen, would you mind if I tried to ride her?" I asked. "Sure, go ahead," was her answer. I got a very unfamiliar feeling in the pit of my stomach. I was scared. In business, I am fearless. Virtually nothing intimidates me, but here was this black horse, simultaneously resurrecting both the fear and confidence of youth.

On a cold spring day, my husband Rick and daughter Katie went with me to the stable to watch me negotiate with Lacey for the first time. I tried to get on while she danced around, throwing her head and backing all around the arena. With the help of Helen, I got on. Although I felt her power beneath me, every fiber of her body seemed filled with fear. She was wound so tight; I wondered what had happened to make this creature tremble at the slightest provocation. I felt compelled to try again. For the next month, I kept going back, trying to get her to trust and to get her to submit because I had gained her confidence, not because of intimidation.

During that month, an amazing thing happened. My forty-five year old muscles remembered and their strength came back. Better than that, the fear subsided, both Lacey's and mine. We connected. We bonded. It was wonderful.

A new fear began. "I'm really growing attached to Lacey," I told my husband. "Helen is thinking of selling her. I don't think I can keep riding her if that's going to happen. It will be too hard to let her go." My husband uncharacteristically ignored my comments (I am *very* hard to ignore). "Just keep working with her," he said. It's good for you and it's good for Lacey. Stop worrying about what's going to happen in the future." I was a bit miffed at being ignored, but I did continue to ride Lacey. Her wonderful nature that only wanted to please was slowly coming to the surface, and it was beautiful to see.

As she improved, I stopped to reflect upon why this horse was responding so quickly. I had never worked with a horse that had been abused before, and it was clear that Lacey had had a very hard life. I discovered I was just doing the same types of things I did at the office. To me the problems Lacey posed were at their root, management problems, and I instinctively used managerial tools to solve them.

I worked hard to be painstakingly predictable. At the office, I never kill the messenger. I try never to respond with anger to a failed situation; I just look for a solution to the problem and then look for a way to implement that solution. If I become angry at work, I physically remove myself from the situation, and only attempt to deal with it when I become calm. I make sure that I am always perceived as the person who can lead and be depended upon. Those are all qualities a successful manager needs. I just used them to build the trust in a scared animal instead of in a disillusioned and cynical employee.

When I became overly frustrated or angry with Lacey, I got off for the day, and we started over when I was in full charge of my emotions. I always asked her to do the same things in the same way. I always found a way to give her some positive feedback, even for the smallest positive effort.

And what did Lacey do for me? She consumed me. When I was with her I could think about nothing else, worry about nothing else. It took all of me to figure out what my next step should be. Her progress became my reward. It was wonderful to see her trust in me growing. I also sensed that I was becoming a kinder, gentler person, and that this change in personality was spilling over into my personal and professional life.

I also had a personal breakthrough. I saw a parallel of nature in its raw form. We (both people and animals) are creatures of free will. Seldom do we prevail when we try to force others to do things our way. The secret is to transform contrary goals into common goals by identifying and satisfying the needs of both parties. This revelation gave me a litmus test for any action I might take. Would the action I was about to take bring me closer to the realization of common goals?

This test has proved invaluable. There is no maybe, no middle ground. It either does or it doesn't. It just turns out that what are good rules for business are also good rules for life, for only the goals change, not how you reach them.

Now back to my story. On a very snowy evening in March, my husband said something was going on at the stable and that Helen said we needed to come over right away. When we waded through the snow and opened the barn door, there stood Lacey, wrapped in wrapping paper replete with bows and a sign that said Happy Anniversary. "I knew there was something special between you two the first time I saw you ride her," my husband said. Well, okay. I did decide to forgive him for ignoring me when I voiced my concerns, for at the very moment I was complaining, I was apparently already the owner of Lacey the horse. Rick has had a knack over the years for knowing just what I need at the time I need it, even up to and including a four-legged teacher.

And there you have it. Lacey is now a permanent fixture in my life or should I say a constant reminder of how, by being a consistent, kinder, gentler person, all the goals of life become reachable. I am convinced that few things in life can teach us more than the animals that touch our lives. If you want something better than analysis, Yoga, consultants or self-help tapes, buy a four-legged teacher. It's the best investment in peace of mind you'll ever make.

Chapter Sixty-One

Take The Damn Vacation

For many years we never took a family vacation. I was convinced that if we did, chaos in the business would result or worse yet, when we returned there wouldn't be a business.

Finally we took the plunge and left. Our worst fears materialized. Employees fought, resulting in several resignations. Major mistakes made it out the door. Commitments were missed. Programming projects screeched to a halt.

"How do other people do it?" I thought. "Do they hire corporate baby sitters?" I began to conjure up logos for a new fledgling business, *Business Sitters International*. I imagined a large dinosaur, a "Business Barney," beautifully attired in a suit, briefcase at his side, his purple and green silhouette gracing the corporate letterhead. The possibilities raced through my mind. I forced myself, begrudgingly, to think about more mundane solutions.

In my daughter's kindergarten class they had a saying, "You get what you get and you don't make a fuss." I liked it. Was there a way to enforce this rule during my absence? I decided it was time to apply Child Psychology 101 and find out.

Perhaps you think this is a bit harsh. Oh no, it's not. Adults are much worse than children. At least children openly express their aggression, release their frustration, and end up playing nicely together five minutes later. Adults never get back to the "play nicely" part.

It was this revelation that made it possible to leave and get some badly needed time off. I accepted the fact that corporate civility was going to disappear during my absence and childish behavior would soon dominate. I accepted that nothing would get done. I anticipated who would fight and who would resign in anger when they didn't get their way. In response, I started building defenses against these office blights.

I started by assigning leadership roles to certain individuals who had the rank and the strength of character to defuse tense situations. I made sure that employees realized that these individuals were in positions of authority. It might not be my authority, but it was certainly better than nothing.

Next, I reduced the risk that things would go out wrong. We shelved all troublesome projects. Work would continue (I hoped) but no new programs were to be placed in production during my absence. The goal was to merely keep the status quo. It is far easier to explain a delay to a client than to explain a major mistake.

I also used timing to reduce risk. I made sure I planned my vacation for the slowest time of the month, when very little output made its way out the door. What could be done early, was done early. What could be delayed, would wait until I returned.

Although I longed for the advantages of a larger corporate structure where the senior management tier can collectively function as a pseudo CEO, I accepted that our smaller size precluded such a solution. We had middle managers who could direct projects, not drive them, enforce procedures, not devise them.

I also had to make some mental adjustments of my own. I had to become comfortable with the thought that the dress code would go out the window, chatting would become the number one priority of many employees, and anyone brave enough would be out of the office each day by three o'clock. Was time away from the office worth this "cost" of doing business? Yes, I decided, it was. I accepted these costs just as I did the cost of the plane ticket.

Having done these things, we packed our bags and left. Were things great when we returned? No, but things weren't as bad as they had been when we returned from previous vacations.

For starters, no one quit. I found intervention by the designated leader at least stopped tempers from flaring to the point where someone actually walked out. Also, no major mistakes made it out the door. Actually, almost nothing made it out the door, but I cheerfully accepted this and handled the explanations of delays that resulted. I remained overjoyed that there was nothing serious to mop up. For the most part, two weeks elapsed without incident and I came back feeling that at least a few of the entrepreneurial chains had been severed. Leaving certainly had its price, but at least it was occasionally affordable.

I still haven't given up on the Business Barney idea. I think it has a lot of merit. Who knows? One day you may get a letter in the mail offering you the services of a very cute (and properly attired) green and purple dinosaur.

Chapter Sixty-Two

Feeling A Little Stressed? Buy Some Fish

My father mentioned periodically that he thought he would like to get some fish. He had read that watching fish has a very calming effect and can be very therapeutic. I wish he had lived longer for many reasons. One of them is to tell him that although I appreciate his many good ideas, THIS WAS NOT ONE OF THEM!

My daughter wanted a gerbil. I put my foot down. "There will be no rodents in the Arend house," I said. "You have a dog. That's good enough." "But the dog is for the whole family," Katie said. "I want something that is just mine." Now had she been an employee, that would have been the end of the discussion. As her supervisor, I had given my final answer and that should have been that. But, because she is The Daughter, and frequently ignores my obvious authority (maybe being an entrepreneur is easier than being a parent) she persisted. I found a solution to the problem. At Petsmart I found a large display of boxes. "Everything you need to set up your own aquarium," it displayed. "Video included to make setup easy, $50.00." I love elegant solutions, and I smugly exited the store with my pet problem solved.

On Christmas morning Katie opened the box. Everyone was excited. We popped the video into the VCR. Well, maybe there were a few things that were not in the box. We returned to Petsmart, where we purchased gravel, a castle for the fish to play in, plastic seaweed, a fish net, fish food, a colorful plastic background scene to glue to the back of the tank, and of course four fish. We had spent a mere $45.50 more and were now ready to go.

We came home with our plastic bag of fish and placed them in their new enhanced environment. Katie's uncle called to congratulate her on starting a fish tank. As a "fish expert" he offered all kinds of advice. "I only feed my fish every couple of days," he said. This was a problem. His advice contradicted the video, which said fish should be fed twice a day. "Let's go back to Petsmart," I said. We need reference books. While there, we purchased two books for $34.50 and a fish tank vacuum for $15.99.

The fish book told us that the tank would have to cycle. This means that the urine excreted by the fish needs to build up in the new tank, causing a temporarily toxic condition which bacteria introduced into the tank balance, given enough time. How do we determine how toxic the water is? With a water testing kit of course! We returned to Petsmart. For $23.97 we bought two water testing kits, one for ammonia and one for pH, and also a bacteria starter kit to speed the cycling process along.

Several days elapsed. The fish did not look well. One was floating on its side. The ammonia level was dangerously high. I couldn't sleep. My worries about the business paled in comparison to my concern about the fish. All the fish had names. Jeff, Bob, and Jack were still holding their own, but we were very worried about Chris, who was floating sideways. The book said this was definitely not a good sign. The book also said that if you have one sick fish, isolate him immediately to prevent infecting the other fish by placing him in a special hospital tank.

We went back to Petsmart. We bought a small two-gallon tank, a small piece of plastic seaweed, three types of fish antibiotics and special antibiotic fish food. We also bought a small tank heater and a small thermometer to stick on the side of the tank. Temperature is critical to the well being of fish, the book had told us. We felt really prepared. After all, it was only another $69.22 and we knew we were doing the right thing.

We placed Chris in his own tank. He looked at us sideways through the glass. He started to swim upside down. We checked the temperature. It was too high! We were cooking poor Chris. I ran and got the heater box. Do not use on tanks smaller than ten gallons, it read. I brought all my problem solving skills to bear and came up with a solution. I took my desk lamp out of my office and placed it six inches above the fish tank. Every hour we returned to check the temperature. Eighty degrees and holding. We had done it! The next day, poor Chris lay lifeless on the bottom of his hospital tank. Despite our heroic efforts, we had failed. We had a small funeral for Chris in the backyard. We were not going to flush *our* fish down any toilet. He clearly deserved a proper burial.

Back in the main tank cycling had begun. The filter however, did not appear to be working and debris was evident all over the tank. We used our extensive research library to find a solution, which now included *Fish for Dummies*, which seemed appropriately named on several levels. Petsmart of course had a number of the recommended power filter choices. We selected one for tanks up to thirty gallons and purchased a good supply of replaceable filters for $40.98. We installed the filter on the tank. It began to whir. The water began to churn. "Look at it pick up that debris!" I said. "It's awesome!" The little fish were flapping their fins furiously. "They look like salmon swimming up stream, Mommy," said Katie. "They'll get used to it," I told her.

That night we sprinkled in their food. The current was just too powerful. Try as they might, the poor little fish couldn't catch their food flakes. We turned off the filter. The debris settled to the bottom of the tank. "Tomorrow we will go back to Petsmart," I said.

The advisory council at Petsmart, with whom we were now well acquainted, suggested the "mini" power filter model. The replaceable filters for the old filter didn't fit this one of course, so we had to buy a good supply of new "mini" filters. The Petsmart people felt sorry for us. "At least the filters are on special," they said. "Ten percent off." We paid $25.18 after our discount.

Life in the big tank started to improve. The debris slowly cleared up and all the fish continued to swim right side up. Algae was becoming a problem, but we were not worried. Did I say not worried? After consulting the book I discovered that severe algae can impair the breathing of fish. It must be stopped! And that's how we wound up getting Speedy the snail. For $1.10 we got our little friend who likes to eat algae. Now however, there is not enough algae in the tank to keep him going so I microwave zucchini slices for him, which I put in his seashell clamp that sticks to the side of the tank. (Only $3.95 at Petsmart.)

I am so glad we got those fish. During the time we were solving our fish problems, I hardly worried about the business at all. If you really feel compelled to find a way to divert your mind from the worries of running a business, I can highly recommend buying fish. In fact, fish can make you learn to really relish going to the office. During our fish adventure, I could not wait to get back to work, just to get a break from watching the fish hour after hour, for signs of new symptoms.

CHAPTER SIXTY-THREE

THE ONE HOUR DAY

When you manage a business, your time is not your own. Each day is composed of hundreds of problem solving moments. Everyone in your organization makes demands on your time, and you can count your day successful if you managed to keep most of these people on track.

All during my childhood, I remember getting up and wandering into the living room where I would see my dad, cigar in hand, reading by the soft light of a lamp in an otherwise dark house. No matter how early I arose, he was always there, sometimes sitting quietly in the shadows, but more often with a book in his lap, just reading away. He used to say he did his best thinking at 5:00 a.m. Not being a morning person, I thought he was nuts. Why would anyone intentionally leave their nice toasty covers so they could sit up in a cold house and think? I often thought wanting to get up at that hour every day was probably a symptom of some sort of sleep disorder.

Twenty years passed. I started a business and grew to know intimately the frustration of never being able to get anything done. It seemed everyone managed my time except me. The steadily increasing pressure eventually started to affect my sleep. I would lie in bed in the early morning, thinking about everything I needed to get done or mulling over an overwhelming problem. Eventually, I got out of bed and started writing TO DO lists and jotting down notes.

I did not see the parallel with my father however, even though I had turned into a closet early morning worker. I frequently would sneak back to bed and polish off one last hour of sleep before re-rising. Sneaky or not, an interesting thing started to occur. My productivity started to go through the roof. In that one hour period each day, I was getting things accomplished that *I* really wanted to get done. I wasn't answering questions or putting out fires. I was doing real problem solving, deciding how to move the business forward and tackling tough strategic problems.

I started going to bed earlier. I started to guard my precious little hour. If my daughter arose too early and wandered into my office, I was not loving, inviting Mommy. Instead, I uncharacteristically waved her out, mumbling something about it wasn't good for little girls to get up before the sun did. I couldn't get her back to bed fast enough.

I am no longer confused by my father's nocturnal behavior. He clearly had learned the secret of the one hour day. In my one little hour, I often feel I have accomplished more than I do in the eight plus hours subsequently logged at the office. There is something about a quiet, darkened house that makes you feel secure and protected. It is where you can try on new, unconventional ideas for size without fear of repercussion. It is where you can stretch your limits by reading books that educate you, make you think, and challenge your ideals. It is where you can review how you plan to spend your day and make a list of things that can really make a difference in your productivity.

Entrepreneurs must be their own cheerleaders, their own problem solvers, and their own strategic planners. In New Age terms, one might say that adopting the one hour day keeps you centered. It does a heck of a lot more than that. It keeps your business afloat, your ideas fresh, and your technical skills sharp. It's also a great way to be around to see some fantastic sunrises.

Adopting the one hour day is better than getting an assistant or business advisor, hiring a marketing consultant, or working with a personal trainer. It gets you back in control of your life in many ways and lets your company profit from the most talented person on the payroll, you.

CHAPTER SIXTY-FOUR

THE NEXT BEST THING TO BEING THERE

It is often difficult for entrepreneurs to leave the office. This is because romper room is alive and well in every business. As soon as the teacher leaves the room, Internet surfing begins, chatter reaches 110 decibels and every petty argument brewing behind the scenes, surfaces anew.

The good news is that there are high-tech ways to minimize the destruction. Leaving the office behind can be painless. Just make sure you stay connected to your office, or in the vernacular of the Sci Fi series Star Trek, to your star ship, with a few 21st century tools. Taking advantage of technology is a great way to insure both your ship's survival and your own peace of mind. Not a bad deal for a captain who never feels she can leave the bridge.

Your "tri-corder" is your laptop. With this simple device you can read your e-mail and remain informed of business issues as they occur. If you don't like what you see, you can use a "sub-space radio frequency" (your cell phone) to issue orders from Star Fleet Command (your hotel room) to get things back on track. If circumstances reach catastrophic proportions, you can "beam" yourself back (get on a return flight by flying standby) and once again take control of your ship before mutiny occurs or the Federation disintegrates (you lose one or more major accounts).

What works for Captain Janeway can work for you. You still remain the captain, you are simply on an away mission, communicator in hand.

When I leave the office without taking along my electronic tethers, my imagination dreams up doomsday office scenarios that would make the strongest CEO quake. I promptly become convinced that we have lost our biggest customer and that twenty percent of the staff plan to tender their resignation upon my return. It is fear of the unknown that is my worst enemy.

Being away from the office while maintaining a virtual connection however, reduces my stress in very real terms. My 21st century tools allow me to monitor e-mails. I know exactly who is happy and who is not. I know which clients are in need of emergency care. If I feel like participating, I can e-mail a suggestion or two. (Are there really any entrepreneurs who can actually refrain from voicing an opinion?) In the mean time, I know what is happening and who or what is driving the process. If a customer is not getting adequate service, or has become angry over a performance issue, I know instantly and can quickly pick up my communicator to e-mail or call him and save the day.

And how long does it take to get and stay plugged in? Surprisingly, very little time. I can pull e-mails and issue orders, just like I was still on the bridge of the *Enterprise*, in roughly an hour a day. That leaves me twenty-three hours to pursue my mission, unfettered by concerns over what might be transpiring back on board ship. The sense of control that knowledge of circumstance brings is absolutely wonderful.

Worry is a constant in the life of most entrepreneurs. Most of us have raised worry beyond mere preoccupation, to a high art form that only business owners can hope to attain. When you are paid to worry you lose your amateur status as a worrier. You worry, therefore you are. It's just another part of the entrepreneurial persona. You do not run the business, you are the business, seven days a week, twenty-four hours a day.

If you can successfully focus on other responsibilities when circumstances require you to be out of the office, you have achieved something very few entrepreneurs can boast about. Most stay imprisoned in a jail of their own construction, deceptively furnished with modular furniture to disguise its true purpose.

Just remember you can bail yourself out from time to time. All it takes are a few high-tech tools that today, are more than just a Star Trek fantasy.

SURVIVAL OF
THE SMARTEST

Chapter Sixty-Five

Employee Power

There are times when even the best run companies experience calamity. Whether such an event merely injures a company or ultimately overwhelms it, depends upon how the person at the helm shares the news and plans the escape.

About seven years ago, we lost our three biggest clients in a ninety-day period. One company was bought out, one went bankrupt, and a third took their billing in-house. All three losses occurred without warning and when we examined what their departure would mean to our bottom line, we realized we would be running at a deficit for at least six months.

I called everyone into the conference room to announce the news. "Well," I said, "we just lost our top three accounts. This sudden loss of revenue means we will now be running in the red by a considerable margin. We have a war chest of cash for emergencies however, and if we sell like crazy and watch expenses, it should be enough to see us through." I took a moment to look around the room. Everyone appeared to be in shock. "I can't do anything about what happened, but there is one thing I *can* do. I can make you a promise. If, at any time, I don't believe we are going to make it, I promise I will warn you, so you can go out and get other jobs. You have my word on it."

After my announcement, people needed time to digest the news. No one said anything for a long time. Slowly a buzz started around the room. It was the product of a bunch of sidebar conversations on how to cut costs and how to get more business quickly. Far from being passive, people were actually taking ownership of the problem and thinking of ways to help solve it!

When bad things happen to a company, they really happen to the people *in* the company. Employees, as well as owners, often feel violated, angry, and betrayed. They want to get back. They also want to *fight* back. Don't ignore these emotions. Instead, acknowledge that the injury occurred and help facilitate the healing process. Begin by being honest and open. Tell the truth and ask for help.

Making employees privy to the coping process spawns the type of innovative problem solving that is desperately needed during a recovery. Even if suggestions are never implemented, involvement conveys the message that both employee knowledge and suggestions are worthy of respect.

During the months that followed, I routinely involved employees in belt-tightening discussions. Far from being threatened, the participants felt empowered because they were part of the process. They also found out that belt-tightening did not always translate into firing people. It also meant not replacing people who left voluntarily, reducing medical and dental benefits, reducing hours of operation, curtailing travel, and leasing rather than purchasing equipment.

I look back with pleasure on our lost-client calamity. During the six months it took us to recover, not one person resigned. One day I commented about how pleased I was that everyone had stuck it out. They let me know why. "We were so relieved to know what the real story was. We all knew what we were up against right from the beginning and that it was going to take all of us to turn things around."

The help needed to overcome a calamity tends to be a lot closer than most entrepreneurs think. Often, it is no farther away than the office phone directory.

CHAPTER SIXTY-SIX

COLLECTIONS—A JOB YOU LOVE TO HATE

Humans certainly understand giving excuses. We all have fond memories of our own versions of "The dog ate my homework," or "What vase?" from our childhoods.

Those who work in the business world quickly become familiar with a unique brand of excuses that offer reasons for nonpayment. Among these are a number of well-known favorites. "The person who signs the checks is out of town. We have a question about the bill and I am not authorized to pay anything until the issue is resolved. The check has been sent on for signature. The invoice is scheduled for next week's or month's check run. We never received that invoice." And finally, the ever-popular excuse, "I'm sure we paid that one; let me check and get back to you."

Unfortunately, as a sufferer of the believer's syndrome, most of these excuses work exceedingly well on me. A customer once told me she didn't get her bill on four consecutive occasions and after repeatedly resending it, it finally dawned on me (duh!) that she was never going to "get" the bill.

After weeks of trying and finally getting through to a CEO who was four months behind in payments, I let him hang up with, "Do you mind if I call you back? My other line is ringing and I've got to pick it up, I'm waiting for an important call."

Here however, is the pathetic part of the story. I was doing collections for my own billing company! If we chose to withhold services, our client's cash flow stopped. I held in my hands the world's best hammer to make someone pay. It was almost as effective as being able to hold their children ransom, but did I use it? No!

Despite my inadequacies, I eventually developed a response to all these excuses. I started with an apology. "I'm sorry to hear that. Unfortunately, our system automatically puts you on "accounting hold" if your account becomes past due. Your data will be processed (insert an equivalent phrase to suit your business) but nothing will be sent out until your account is brought current. Please advise us when that will be so we can put you back on the processing schedule." It sounds so simple, but it is so, so hard to do.

I find it particularly hard to stick to my guns when there is culpability of some sort on our side. Perhaps we weren't quite as timely as we could have been on a request. Perhaps something wasn't implemented properly. Instead of giving the client a small concession to compensate for the problem and demanding payment on the bulk of the invoice, I frequently have allowed the client to receive full services while they racked up three or four months worth of charges as we argued the point.

I have learned from experience that if payments get more than three months behind, the money will never materialize. They are not fighting hard because they don't think they should pay (regardless of what they say), they are refusing to pay because they have serious financial problems that they cannot overcome.

If they go bankrupt, your problem gets even worse. Expenses incurred before the date of a bankruptcy filing are referred to as pre-petition debt. By filing for bankruptcy, the filing company no longer has to pay this already incurred debt. Instead, the debt gets added together with all other debt the company incurred prior to the filing date, and a judge administers a plan for equitable distribution of available funds to all creditors. Unless you are a secured creditor, forget it. You will, at best, get pennies on the dollar, it will take forever, and your attorney's fees will probably exceed what you get anyway.

So, what have I learned the hard way? Make them pay now. Make them pay all of it. Do not listen to their sob stories. Use whatever hammer you have by withholding services and do it early! Do not let your fear of losing or irritating your clients affect the actions you take to collect money. That is often what they are counting on.

I still find it exceedingly hard to do this myself and I still mess up by allowing certain clients to slide when I hear a particularly compelling sob story, but hey, I'm the one who believed the postman couldn't find an address on four consecutive occasions.

CHAPTER SIXTY-SEVEN

EXCUSES THAT WORK

In every business, cash makes the world go round. Businesses do not go under because they're in the red; they go out of business because they run out of cash. And how do you insure you will not run out of cash? A good way is to become adept at payables management.

To illustrate, let's assume there is a cash crisis. (This is not much of a stretch for most small businesses.) When cash is tight, the first step on the road to effective payables management is to always follow the payables hierarchy.

The hierarchy goes like this:

1. Payroll

2. Utilities

3. Credit lines and mortgages

4. Suppliers of cost-of-goods-sold inventory

5. Taxes

6. All other payables

PAYROLL

Payroll deserves serious attention because it is often the biggest single cost of doing business. Even though there is no way to avoid this expense, you can still artfully approach how you fund your payroll and significantly ease the cash flow burden it creates.

Although manually cutting checks is a little less expensive and gives you ultimate control over your payroll expenditure, the best, most cost effective way to manage payroll is to use a payroll service. We use a service that rids us of the headaches of calculating payroll and submitting taxes, yet only costs a couple of hundred dollars a month. Just to give you an idea of how important it is, I think it's better than a body massage. In fact, I would much rather have a payroll service than a masseuse!

Regardless of whether or not you use a service, the first thing to realize about payroll is that the cost of it can be covered in stages. Typically, taxes come out the day before payroll checks are cut. As you start to fund the payroll, deposit only enough to cover the tax amount. Deposit nothing more until the payroll checks arrive from the payroll company.

Establish a corporate policy that states checks will only be distributed after 3:00 p.m. This guarantees that nothing will clear the day checks are distributed. A good policy is to cover twenty percent of the payroll the first day. This protects you from the occasional desperate employee who presents his check at your bank for payment. (It actually does happen.) Next, call the bank each day to see how fast people deposit their checks. Typically you will find that most checks clear on day three or four while the last twenty percent of checks clear on day seven to ten.

Being able to predict how fast checks clear is a huge weapon because it allows you to transfer funds to your payroll account in step with the need. When you are fighting for cash flow, this knowledge is incredibly important. Timing alone can make all the difference in a truly serious cash crisis.

It goes without saying that as an owner, your own check should always be held until adequate cash is available to cover the whole payroll. During an extremely severe cash crisis, you should remove yourself from the payroll altogether. This way, no taxes will be calculated for your check and the total tax hit for the pay period will be reduced.

Payroll deserves serious attention, not only because it represents a large recurring expense, but also because it is an expense you can adjust to immediately improve the bottom line. Payroll expense can be reduced by offering employees reduced work schedules, time off without pay, and by encouraging marginal people to quit.

Tight management of your payroll expense is well worth the effort. Most of the time, you are rewarded by being able to slide through without cutting any full time jobs. Avoiding layoffs should be one of your premier objectives, because a layoff *of any size* sends waves of negativity through your organization. Watch payroll like a hawk. Tweak and dance as required. Repeat monthly if necessary.

UTILITIES

Utilities are second in the hierarchy of payables for several reasons. First, you cannot mess with a utility. They will shut you off and if they do, they will require a deposit before they restore service and will charge you a hefty reconnection fee as well. Second, since you have to keep utility bills relatively current anyway, you might as well do so religiously so that you will always have at least a few good credit references at your disposal. This is a wonderful strategy, because unless you really trash your credit, the existence of a couple of stellar credit references will always allow you to obtain other sources of credit.

Make sure you flag utilities in your payables system and *always* pay them before they send disconnect notices. Once disconnect notices have been issued, you may find yourself on the "accounts to watch" list which will shorten the time you have to pay. It goes without saying that they will no longer be any good as credit references.

CREDIT LINES AND MORTGAGES

Third on the hierarchy list is credit lines and mortgages. Banks, the benevolent holders of these credit devices, can cause a lot of trouble. They can freeze accounts, place liens on assets, call notes and hold deposits. They are very, *very* dangerous. Don't set up credit lines unless absolutely necessary. If you must, make sure they are paid according to all the terms in the agreement and pay them *on time.*

There are not enough hours in the day to cope with all the problems banks can cause if they are not paid timely. Here's the good news. They are basically powerless to do anything if you are fulfilling your contractual commitments. They can fume and roar and say they have all sorts of options, but it's really just a lot of hot air. If you need to, take money out of your kid's college fund, hock some jewelry, sell some stock, do whatever it takes. Just make sure you pay the damn bank.

SUPPLIERS OF COST-OF-GOODS-SOLD INVENTORY

The fourth item on the list is cost-of-goods-sold payables. These vendors must be paid because they furnish the raw materials needed to produce your products and services. In our business, paper vendors fall into this category. We cannot print a bill without paper, so if we go on credit-hold with these guys, we're dead.

There is a way out, however. If you are a good customer in terms of volume with a vendor, you can frequently negotiate extended payment terms. In a true cash crisis, the last thing you should worry about is being hit with finance charges. Disregard any charge a delayed payment schedule may cost you and accept the extended terms cheerfully. In some instances, I have agreed to pay ridiculous interest charges or late fees in exchange for a positive credit report. This is worthwhile because cost-of-goods-sold vendors are great to put on credit applications due to the high credit limits normally associated with these accounts. Credit is just virtual cash, and in the war to remain solvent, worthy of aggressive pursuit.

So what do you do if you really get into trouble and can't pay your cost-of-goods-sold vendors? In a best case scenario, you see this coming and use existing vendors to secure several other "replacement" vendors before your slow payment history taints your credit report. Otherwise, when the pressure is on, go directly to the vendor you owe a ton of money to and explain your cash crisis. Make sure the story you give is plausible, has a truthful center and a happy ending. Due to the serious damage cost-of-goods-sold vendors stand to incur from your default, you will often be pleasantly surprised by their willingness to cooperate and compromise.

We routinely pursue clients legally when they fail to pay their bill. Often they default due to severe financial problems. Sometimes they are just scummy people who try to get out of paying at the end of their contract. Based on the existence of these pending awards, I sometimes tell creditors that a large customer has refused to pay, and that we are involved in arbitration and expect a judgment shortly. I explain that we understand they may want to limit our credit, but that we still plan to pay them off on a slow but steady schedule until we receive a judgment allowing us to pay them off in full. Because we almost always have some sort of litigation in progress, this statement is accurate.

A forthright approach like this is good because it will typically: prevent you from being sent to collections, keep your business in the water by keeping you supplied with critical inventory items, and buy you a significant amount of time to work through your cash crisis. (From juggling vendors in this manner, you can easily add six months to your available cash life.)

TAXES

A tax payable is an amazingly flexible payable. With rare exception (payroll taxes) most tax payments can be significantly delayed. Property taxes are a good example. Often you can elect to pay these taxes after the scheduled date for a small increase in amount. Sometimes the interest earned on money during the delayed payment interval exceeds the amount of extra interest charged! If you find yourself struggling with cash, examine the payment terms associated with each tax you must pay. You may find several options that will really help you stretch your dollars for a minimal cost.

ALL OTHER PAYABLES

The final category in the payables hierarchy is "other" payables. These vendors may get angry but the services or products they provide are not necessary to keep the doors open. Attorneys and accountants, office supply companies, and cleaning and courier services are all examples of this type of payable.

Although you do need to take their invoices seriously, there are several things you can do to help stretch out credit terms with these vendors. Little bitty payments, as long as they keep coming, will generally keep these creditors at bay. There is no question that honesty is the best policy with these people. I usually take the tack that we are trying to be fair to all vendors in these "hard times" and everyone else is getting a like pittance. Misery loves company and it appears this rule certainly applies to vendors. When they hear of our dilemma and of our attempt to pay off everyone ratably, they seldom cause problems. Vendors respond very favorably to the concept of equitable treatment of creditors and I have never found any instance of retaliation when we were at least paying each vendor something.

The absolute worst thing you can do is to ignore vendor calls. They will respond by turning you over to a collection company whose employees will make your life miserable and ruin your credit rating. Not only will they pester you and destroy your credit, they will suck down the morale of everyone in your accounting department. Why spend energy ignoring past due vendors when it takes so little to take the pressure off? Just get your spiel down so you can deliver your speech effectively and get ready for things to improve.

The idea behind these suggestions is not just to stave off the wolves while you go deeper in debt. The purpose of managing payables creatively is to allow you time to come up with a way to balance expenses and revenue and actually *solve* your cash crisis.

If you follow the steps above, you will be well armed for your next financial crunch. Just use the steps judiciously and remember, they do not solve anything that is wrong in your business. They only buy you time.

Chapter Sixty-Eight

Don't Make Sales The Step Child

What is sales? In my mind, sales and plaid jackets are still linked. Salespeople are also who you avoid during the dinner hour. I guess I have never been very clear on the intricacies of selling; it's just not my thing.

When my business started, I expected that somehow sales would just happen. I had some sense that it was necessary to have a sales force, but I didn't like the typical sales personality. I found it distasteful. It was so much more pleasant dealing with people like myself, who reveled in the technical world of bits and bytes.

Fortunately, the gods smiled upon us and we eked along and gained business primarily by networking our connections in the industry. Life was precarious however, and at a certain size it became evident that we were merely treading water. To actually grow, we needed to welcome sales into the family.

Several times during our corporate history we had tried to hire someone to lead the sales charge and each time it was a disaster. What we failed to adequately factor in was that we were hiring "salespeople." Because those we interviewed often could sell themselves despite their inability to sell other things, we failed to see through their rhetoric and kept getting "sold" people who could not perform.

Eventually, it became obvious that we needed help from a higher power. It was time to get someone involved whose opinion could be trusted and who would be detached enough from the operations of the business to help us define and assemble a viable sales and marketing plan.

What changed the course of our business was the addition of outside perspective. We found help by joining a group called TAB (The Alternative Board). The concept behind this group is simple. Many small to medium sized businesses do not have the resources to hire a formal board of directors. This does not mean these businesses don't need advice. It only means that a traditional board is beyond their financial reach.

We were just such a business. After the death of my father, we recognized we had no detached, outside source of advice. TAB gave us both one-on-one consulting and access to a group of like individuals, who functioned as a sounding board for problems.

On a monthly basis, the CEOs of a dozen companies (including ours) got together and talked about their problems in a round table discussion. Advice was given and progress tracked. A paid consultant mediated the discussions and consulted with us privately as well.

Our mediator, Mike, was a successful entrepreneur whose focus during his own career had been sales. His sales perspective was just what we needed to help shed some light on what was lacking in our approach to sales and marketing.

What ultimately became obvious was that we had failed to dedicate resources to that which we did not clearly understand. We couldn't successfully hire a sales director, so we did without. We didn't have a clear vision of the tools needed to advance our marketing ideas, so we did nothing. We didn't understand that the sales process could be systematized, just like any other corporate function, so we continued to operate without procedures or controls.

What happened following Mike's involvement was the implementation of all the missing pieces. Sales had been the stepchild because we did not understand the needs of the child. We started at the beginning. We started by defining sales.

Here is a very useful definition for those of you, who like me, are easily confused over the difference between sales and marketing. Sales is the engine of the car. Marketing is the steering wheel.

We started with the steering wheel. Obviously, we first needed to decide where we wanted to go. Mike played the role of facilitator. We had the knowledge and ability to analyze both marketing opportunities and our strengths and weaknesses, but we needed someone to help us navigate through the process. Once we began, the process became self-generating. We agreed upon market opportunities we wished to explore. We implemented plans to conduct research to evaluate the opportunities we identified. We actually devoted resources (both human and financial) to finding the answers we needed. We hadn't started the car yet, but we had found the ignition!

Next, we turned our hand to sales. We put in incentive programs. We made sure salary structures kept our sales people hungry enough to insure at least minimal performance. Finally, we put in measures and milestones. We had grown weary of the lies. Now we could track phone calls made, demonstrations conducted, and proposals submitted. We assembled weekly to publicly evaluate our progress and chastise those who were not keeping pace. We learned that sales is not magic. It's just another part of the business that deserves resources and attention, management and procedures, accolades and criticism.

What historically had been misunderstood, and for the most part ignored, became a vital part of the business. Being technically based meant that we were never at risk of being sales *controlled* (perish the thought!) but we were learning we needed to be sales driven. We had a Maserati, but historically it had a four cylinder engine and we steered it by leaning from side to side. Now we had twelve cylinders and a real leather steering wheel. It finally dawned on us that our business had been a good looking vehicle with nowhere to go. We were now equipped. It was time for a road trip.

The first year sales became empowered and was no longer treated as a stepchild became our most successful sales year on record. Not only did we sell more, but we qualified the sales we made, insuring that the companies we agreed to serve were financially viable. This was definitely a good thing, for the worst blows we have been dealt over our twenty-year history have been from the unexpected bankruptcies of clients.

We are indebted to Mike for helping us focus on the stepchild of our business. We all tend to gravitate toward the areas we find comfortable, but in a small business showing favoritism can be fatal. Bigger businesses have well defined departments with the strength to compete against each other for limited resources. Smaller businesses do not. As the leader of a smaller business, you alone must balance the resources and put aside your predispositions for certain business areas through sheer will power.

Never let sales become the stepchild of your business. If you are predisposed, as I am, to make it a stepchild, by all means get help. The world is full of people smarter than you are, and all you have to do to get their help is ask. Okay, the help may not be *free*, but then even a Maserati's top speed is zero until you spring for the gas.

CHAPTER SIXTY-NINE

REAL-LIFE POKER

My husband is fond of saying to me, "Please don't play poker, we just can't afford it." He then points out with relish that every opinion I ever had can easily be discerned from my face. Okay, so my motives are seldom disguised, and I should stick to playing Solitaire.

Occasionally however (did I really say occasionally?), I disagree with my husband's opinion. I think sometimes I *should* play poker, at least in business. Not only has experience taught me when to hold'em and when to fold'em, it has also taught me how to play people when they are fervently trying to play me. I may not naturally possess a poker face but I have learned how to don one, from years of practice in the business world. I can highly recommend acquiring this business skill to anyone but particularly to women in business, for those who learn to mask their intentions can often prevail against even the most unscrupulous opponent.

So, how does this poker face stuff work? It begins with acknowledging that in the higher ranks of business, ego is still king. Senior managers commonly suffer from the delusion that they are far smarter and have more business savvy than everyone else. They feel dominant over men of lesser rank. They often feel positively omnipotent over women, regardless of rank. It is this sense of supremacy that provides us allegedly weaker foes with our advantage. If we play our cards right, we can parlay even the weakest of business cards into a winning hand.

In the late 80's, we had a customer who was having financial trouble. The bane of our existence as a service company has been companies unable to pay their bills, so this was nothing new to us. What was new, was that the owners of the company were unscrupulous.

They began by making promises to pay they never intended to keep. They told us they had business arrangements that either didn't exist or fell apart shortly after their creation. They lied about every conceivable aspect of their business in order to manipulate us to their advantage. They tried to coerce us into doing customized programming for which they could not pay. They demanded that we provide them service when they were overextended. They skipped out on other vendors and then tried to trick us into being their unwitting accomplice.

Was I oblivious to what they were trying to do? Not at all. Did I pretend to be oblivious? Absolutely. I adopted the role of "the dumb blond of business" with relish. I wrote letters at every opportunity (see Chapter Fifty Four, *The Power of the Pen*), subtly documenting their motives and manipulations, while I demurred to their every request and remained just dumb enough to convince them I believed what they were telling me.

Slowly we collected a war chest of evidence, while smiling with our corporate toe in the sand and "helping" them through their difficult times. When they finally had to show their cards (they electronically stole a database and simultaneously informed us they were not going to pay us another dime), we had them exactly where we wanted them. Fourteen months later, we all stood before a judge as the evil business boys were forced to hand us a check for $157,000. Gotcha! The meek shall inherit the earth, or in this case, the woman entrepreneur who learned to play poker.

Assuming that someone else is incapable of fighting back, often marks the beginning of the end for the one who assumes. People come in all sizes and packages, and people often make mistakes in their assumptions of others. I try hard never to let my preconceived opinion of someone cause me to believe they are incapable of a real dogfight. What I do to others, I do not want them to be able to do to me!

If confrontation appears to be looming on your horizon, pocket your aggressions for a moment. Sit back and analyze the situation, and figure out how you can position yourself to win before the opposition recognizes you are aware of whatever dishonest or immoral thing they are trying to pull.

Just put on a smile and enjoy watching your opponent learn the hard way, how *real-life* poker is played.

CHAPTER SEVENTY

THE ART OF
COURSE CORRECTION

DEMISE OF A BLUE CHIP

A giant and a name known long,
Dwarfed the Wall Street icons well
And boasted of its mighty wealth,
Until its lofty leaders fell.
Thousands woke without a job,
A downsized legend crashed and died
It saddened hearts when truth revealed,
Its leaders to themselves had lied.

Not even the largest companies are immune from layoffs. And why do massive layoffs become necessary? Because corporate leaders are often too self-absorbed or too scared to react to the writing on the wall six to twelve months earlier, when an appropriate adjustment in course could preclude a massive correction.

Companies don't get into trouble overnight. The telltale signs begin months, or sometimes even years, earlier. Are the people who run these companies really that stupid? No, they are certainly able to analyze data and determine trends. They just have trouble pocketing their egos, overcoming greed and facing reality. As a result, they often don't admit that trouble is brewing, much less do anything about it, until it is *obvious to everyone.*

The lure of big dollars can be overwhelming. Countries have fallen, lovers, parents and children have been betrayed, and wars have begun, all because of greed. Greed is powerful because it is a direct manifestation of insecurity. Somehow we think if we have enough money we can protect ourselves from worldly dangers. Greed is a malignant outgrowth of self-preservation, our highest-order need.

Pride is also tied to self-preservation. We use pride to measure our worth and to justify our desire for self-preservation. It is normally from the affirmations of others that we grow our feeling of pride. It is not hard to understand then, why clearly intelligent people fail to take action when a mountain of data makes clear that action is imperative. They are following their instinct for self-preservation. Moral fiber often succumbs to greed and pride when the money is big enough or the accolades are great enough.

In the business world, overcoming fears of retribution for making decisions that are purely for the corporate good cannot be done by the faint of heart, only by the honest at heart.

Of all of the things instilled by my father, the most important was: Be honest with yourself. Self-preservation matters, but the most important thing to preserve is your self-respect. Making decisions independent of selfish motives is the best way to acquire a sense of pride that cannot be tarnished or taken away by others, because affirmations for doing the right thing, come from within. The added benefit is that empirical decision making will also save your business from the pitfalls experienced at companies where greed and fear rule.

Many examples exist today from which we can learn. The airline industry has been driven into bankruptcy by runaway wage rates driven by years of unbridled labor-union greed. Big companies such as Enron and MCI WorldCom have disintegrated because greedy executives were unwilling to reveal poor corporate performance and decided instead, to misstate financial information. Examples of devastation caused by greed and pride are everywhere.

Be tough enough to take action even when your instincts for self-preservation instill paralysis. Time is seldom on your side in business.

Be brave enough to act while there is still time for your business to react. But above all, do not let your desire for affirmations from others or excessive personal gain, color your decision-making.

Decide what is right using your gut. Decide what to do using the data. For a sense of pride that comes from knowing you did the right thing at the right time, is the sweetest reward of all.

FRONT LINE DEFENSES

CHAPTER SEVENTY-ONE

I THOUGHT YOU HAD THE PASSWORD

"**D**oes anyone remember his dog's name?" I asked. The assembled group looked at their shoes. "I know, let's get his personnel file and look up his birthday. Didn't he have a daughter? What was her name?"

If this conversation sounds familiar, you may have had the pleasure of trying to break into your own computer, voice mail, or firewall system. It typically happens when some technical person either resigns or is fired. Unfortunately, as technology advances, we become more and more dependent on security specialists who often hold the only key to our electronic treasure chest of knowledge.

When Randy, our system administrator resigned unexpectedly, we immediately knew we were in trouble. The relationship he had with most people in the company was strained, and his attempts to keep everything he did secret, had been obvious from the start. When asked direct questions, he always responded with cryptic and evasive answers. Asking for an updated password list was also pointless as the list he produced was always obsolete and conveniently left out his secret "backdoor" passwords. Worst of all, his odd behavior, which included tattooing the insides of his eyelids (somebody *really* needs to explain this one to me), brought into question his stability and caused us to worry about what he might try to do if he no longer worked for the company.

After Randy left, we found we were unable to access our computer's firewall. He had locked us out of it, and of course, only he knew the password. We wanted to use the firewall to keep *him* out. Instead the system he designed kept us out. We spent days trying to hack into our own system. It was humiliating.

It is frightening when you realize that one of your employees can easily hold you hostage in your own business. When I finally woke up to this fact, it made me angry and I vowed to never let it happen again. I armed myself for battle. My weapon of choice was cross-training.

Cross-training is good for a lot of reasons. First, it fosters a sincere appreciation among different work groups for the responsibilities and problems of others. It also shoots down permanently, any one person's attempt to harbor information.

When someone goes through the cross-training process, they must actually perform the job to show they fully understand the function. In the case of security related tasks, they must demonstrate their ability to access a server or firewall, including being able to change a password.

While, at first blush, it may seem contrary to the security interests of the company to equip multiple people with the ability to access sensitive information, it has proven to be far less risky than allowing critical knowledge to be hoarded by a single employee.

Make sure when you institute cross-training in your business that you include yourself. It's your business. You need to make sure you have personal knowledge of the critical components that make it go. Do not make the mistake of assuming you are too busy or too removed from the process to get involved in cross-training. Take the time. It's the cheapest insurance policy you will ever buy.

Below is a list of valuable company assets that should be accessible by multiple people in your business or kept by you personally under lock and key.

1. All user passwords to computer systems you operate.

2. All system passwords.

3. Passwords to external computer systems you must access.

4. Account numbers and access codes for all bank accounts.

5. Current payroll information and instructions for updating the payroll system.

6. Keys for all locks in your office building.

7. All phone numbers and procedures for maintenance contract suppliers.

8. All alarm system codes.

9. A list of all personnel with after hours access e.g. cleaning people.

10. Procedures and passwords for uploading web site information.

11. A list of all personnel possessing building keys.

12. A list of all employees possessing corporate credit cards or phone cards.

13. Methods used by outsiders to access internal computer systems.

14. All IP addresses used by your company.

15. Written documentation detailing your firewall set up if you maintain one.

Make sure designated individuals are required to promptly notify you if any of these items change and verify that the updated code or password information you receive, actually works.

It *is* possible to protect yourself from disgruntled insiders in your business. Cross-train your way to security. It's excellent insurance, and best of all, it's free.

Chapter Seventy-Two

Attacking Problems 101

I have always loved problem solving. Why? Because it is the adrenaline rush of business. Problems are mountains before us begging to be climbed. It is the conquest of these mountains that keeps us hungry for more challenges.

There is no mystique to solving problems. All problems contain the same elements and respond to the same formula. A personnel problem and a customer complaint should both get the same treatment, despite the very different circumstances that may have caused them. The trick is to correctly apply problem solving rules. If you apply the rules correctly, not only will the problem be solved, you will insure that the same problem does not repeat.

Unfortunately, an inability to solve problems and to convey problem solving techniques to others often keeps entrepreneurs chained to their businesses, mopping up mess after mess. The good news is that anyone can learn to follow basic problem solving rules. Adopt the rules yourself, pass them on to your employees, and spring yourself from entrepreneurial jail. The food may be great, but the hours are definitely lousy.

All problems begin with discovery. This brings us to the first rule of problem solving.

Rule one: *Don't Shoot the Messenger.*

Of all the rules, this one is the most important. If you shoot the messenger, messages will cease to arrive. An employee who fears retribution will not bring problems to your attention. Instead, she will try to disassociate herself from the problem, hide it, or pass the buck to someone else. All of these responses are disastrous because each precludes you from intervening promptly to correct the situation.

Rule two: *Determine the scope of the problem.*

There is a big difference between a $50.00 mistake and one costing $50,000.00. No matter how stupid or client affecting, fifty bucks is still only fifty bucks. Start by asking how big, how much, how many; whatever question will ultimately lead to the dollar impact of the problem. Large dollar problems are your cue to quickly turn on the afterburners and go after a solution, or at a minimum, an explanation.

Rule three: *Discover who knows about the problem.*

If the person or customer affected by the problem doesn't know about it, you have a tremendous strategic advantage. There is a huge difference between a problem that you have the luxury to "package" because the party affected is not yet aware of it and a problem that you have been regaled with, at high volume on the phone or in a terse e-mail that cc'd the world. How you respond to a problem is always dictated by the answer to "who knows."

Rule four: *Evaluate the need for legal advice.*

My legal background always leads me to ask this question: Did the party affected cause the problem or did their actions or their failure to act make the problem more difficult to discover and/ or ultimately to solve? (Sorry, a little legaleze slips out every now and then.) A "yes" here can really help you turn the tide on the assignment of blame. If the party affected caused the problem or made it worse, you're saved! You now have at your disposal the tools to manage the situation. If not, you're screwed, and it is time to pull out the stops and call an attorney.

I normally do not represent myself. I let my attorney do his job. If you do not have a legal background and the problem is serious, i.e. potentially large dollars at stake, it is critical that you make a quick call to your lawyer to see how you should position yourself to minimize damage. Not calling to get legal advice is one of the single biggest blunders entrepreneurs make. They fail to bring a legal perspective to the situation until it is too late to make much of a difference. The time to legally maneuver is when the lines of war are being drawn in the sand, not after the battle has started. If it's serious, spend a couple of hundred dollars and make the call.

Rule five: *Create a public relations plan.*

Managing expectations is more important than solving the problem itself. That bears repeating. Worry about expectations before fixing the problem itself. The problem can't sue you, but the person or company affected by the problem can. Once you decide what to say, make sure you personally review and approve whatever communication is sent. You don't get a second chance to make a first impression. Make sure you get it right the first time.

Rule six: *Marshal your forces.*

If you find that your company is solely or partially responsible for the problem, begin to marshal your forces. This means everyone in your company must adopt a problem solving attitude and focus exclusively on fashioning a solution. This is where you must shut down the finger pointing and assignment of blame, particularly if the blame emanates from you. The assignment of blame, even a minor assignment, will impede the solution finding process. You can do a postmortem later.

Start every problem solving meeting with a statement like, "We all know we need to evaluate why this happened and how we can keep it from happening again. Right now, the task at hand is to stop the bleeding, so let's see what we can do to get this thing turned around." Everyone will let out a collective sigh of relief as you make this speech, because they know that finger pointing will not be part of the discussion. After all, when the pressure is on, what you need is a problem-solving machine, not one programmed for self-destruction.

Rule seven: *Resolve the real issue.*

Implement the corrective plan as agreed and monitor it *every step of the way.* All of the effort you expended to manage expectations will be worthless if the problem stays a problem or gets worse. Particularly when the stakes are high, make sure you are the one driving the process. Feeling fairly confident that things will get resolved is not enough. A big problem can bring your company down. Make absolutely sure the plan devised to correct the problem is being implemented.

Rule eight: *Conduct a postmortem.*

Assuming the problem has been addressed and damage control has been performed, it is now time for a postmortem. Everyone involved should be present. Take the personalities out of the equation. Make sure everyone attacks the problem (not their coworkers) and calmly discuss why the problem happened and how to prevent it in the future. Was it carelessness? People will always make mistakes. How is it possible to catch the particular mistake that occurred? Did the client cause the problem? How could that relationship be better controlled to prevent a repeat? Was a procedure lacking or ignored? How can a system be devised to make sure steps are followed in the manner required? Once all of these questions have been answered, it is time to conduct one-on-one discussions.

Rule nine: *Conduct one-on-one discussions.*

If an individual failed to perform adequately and that was the root of the problem, talk to him privately, one-on-one. Talking to him privately preserves the golden rule of management: Always praise people publicly and criticize them privately. By following this rule, you can effect change and preserve egos at the same time.

Attacking problems using this nine-step approach is a way to strengthen your organization by minimizing problems and preventing similar ones from occurring. As my father used to say, "If you can think of a different mistake to make everyday, I won't say a word because that's just a training problem. The first time you repeat, I've got you, because *you* are the problem.

Make your goal "no repeats" and watch your company grow stronger and wiser as you become an organization that really knows how to learn from its mistakes.

CHAPTER SEVENTY-THREE

A LOVE AFFAIR WITH CREDIT CARDS

Credit cards are a marvel of the 20th century. They are probably responsible for more divorces and more addictions than all other things put together. I love them.

Easy credit, which is the nemesis of so many people, has been a good friend to me. Even though occasionally it has gotten the upper hand, I readily acknowledge that much of what I have achieved would not have been possible without my VISA. I never leave home without it.

At age sixteen, my father showed a glimmer of brilliance when he went down to his bank and asked the president, a friend of his, to issue me a VISA card. "Dick," the president said, "are you sure you want to do this? She's only sixteen and you will be responsible for the bill. You're going to have to be a cosigner." "Absolutely," Dad answered. "Just don't tell her I'm on the hook for what she charges." My father presented me with the card. It had a $300.00 limit.

At the time, I had a job selling shoes at a local department store. I worked thirty hours a week, and so, making $1.35 an hour, I had "unlimited" resources. In one month I bought contact lenses, a set of luggage, and a wide variety of clothes from the department store that employed me. It took me less than a month to reach "my limit."

I vividly remember the panic that ensued. Dad didn't say a word. He just let me sweat, as each month I tried to whittle away my debt. It took six months to pay it off. Dad and his banker got their share of chuckles over my lesson in credit. The good news was that it *was* a lesson. I gained a healthy respect for credit and fortunately learned at an early age that I alone evaluated the risks and rewards of my expenditures.

When circumstances first presented an opportunity to take the entrepreneurial plunge, I did not have the resources to start a business. My husband and I both made respectable incomes, but we did not have a bankroll sufficient for striking out on our own. What we did have was a fist full of credit cards.

Would a bank have given us the money to start a new venture? Absolutely not. It was a calculated risk, and our calculations showed it made sense to take the plunge. We believed in us even if the bankers didn't, and guess what? Thanks to credit cards, we didn't have to ask anyone for permission. I went down to the local bank with a fist full of cards and cash advanced every one of them up to the limit. I walked out with slightly over $30,000.00.

My husband retained his high paying job, and I rented office space, bought furniture and set up our fledgling computer services company. By all rights we should have held a small ceremony to pay homage to VISA. Without the credit cards we would have had to present our case to a bank. As many of us know from personal experience, bankers only supply money to those who can get money elsewhere. If a bank is your only option, their policy states that they must say no promptly. Did I say promptly? A tree sloth is quick relative to most bankers. No, banks were certainly not an option for us. How ironic, I thought, that the very cards used to circumvent difficulties in getting a bank loan were furnished by the banks themselves. I guess getting twenty-one percent interest just alters a banker's view of acceptable risk.

Once I fully appreciated the autonomy credit cards could provide, I started pursuing credit card options in earnest. Whenever I received a credit card offer in the mail, I accepted. I also discovered several ways to lower the interest rates I paid, making credit card financing a viable long-term tool.

As virtually everyone knows, introductory credit card offers abound. If your credit is reasonably good, you can opt for these deals and then transfer balances from other cards to take advantage of the three to six month introductory periods. The lesser known method to obtain a lower interest rate is to call the credit card company every ninety days and ask them to lower the rate. In the interest of keeping you as a customer, the answer is usually yes. Contrary to popular belief, repeated calling can result in an interest rate as low as six percent when the standard rate is fifteen.

You cannot do this however, without a credit track record. Typically, you must show an active usage history and a good payment record for at least a year. Invest this time. It's worth it. As an entrepreneur, the battle is always to gain control of the situation. With control typically comes improved profitability or in dire cases, survivability. If you can extend reasonably priced credit to yourself when the need arises without going through a lengthy approval process, you have solved one of the biggest problems facing all entrepreneurs.

Personal credit is easier to get than corporate credit. Just use your personal credit cards for the business. Book the activity as a loan to the business and charge the business the interest as an expense for receiving the loan. Better yet, have the company just treat it as a business credit card by paying everything. No one need know the card is not in the name of the business. Finally, as the business produces a track record of its own, have the business apply for a business credit card so that you are off the hook personally. The clear downside of using personal credit cards for business is that if you have business reversals, you have sucked yourself in personally.

This may not be as bad as it seems, however. Had you gotten a loan from the bank directly, you would have been required to either cosign or guarantee the loan anyway. It's just that personal credit card debt is a little nearer and dearer to everyone's heart, and a problem paying a card can really torpedo your personal credit—not a good thing.

Much has been written about the abuse of credit cards. It continues to be one of our country's biggest blights and continues to spin out of control. I was lucky. I had a father who took steps to make sure I learned about the judicious use of credit and honed my skills in self-restraint. If you were not so lucky, it's still not too late. Credit counseling abounds. In my opinion it is well worth mastering the credit genie. No other tool can serve you as well to meet the unexpected cash crises that are all too familiar to entrepreneurs.

CHAPTER SEVENTY-FOUR

AND BABY BANK
MAKES THREE

There is no such thing as a perfect bank. This statement is not quite accurate. Let me amend it. There is no such thing as a good bank. Oops, let me try again. There is no such thing as an okay bank. Gee, that's still not right. That just leaves ....

Bankers are notoriously the tenuous component of business. They are critical to every entrepreneur, yet forging a stable and lasting relationship that can survive good times and bad is practically impossible. It is this fact that forces you to adopt a defensive posture when dealing with banks so that you, and not your banker, ultimately control the destiny of your business.

The fickleness of banks makes the following corollary imperative. Make sure you always maintain banking relations with at least three banks, and make sure one of the three is "a baby."

Why should one of the banks be a baby? Because small banks operate using different rule sets than large banks. Decision making occurs locally, which, if you have more than the average allotment of charm and finesse, can mean the difference between approval and unceremonious rejection.

Small banks also love to help the underdog, particularly when one of the big banks has refused to help. When situations become financially difficult, small banks are less likely to act adversely to your interests.

Their relatively small loan base makes your account more important to them than it would be to a larger financial institution.

Although it is often possible to get small banks to back you when large banks will not, all sizes of banks share one thing in common. When any of them smell serious trouble, they will drop you like a hot potato and you will not be given enough time to forge a new banking relationship before the old one disintegrates. This is why you must maintain at least three banking relationships concurrently.

Small bank relationships are kept alive through personal contact. Large bank relationships are maintained almost exclusively through information exchange. Each month, big banks pop your numbers into their formulas and then let you know if the bank wishes to "continue the relationship."

Do not, under any conditions, become lulled into thinking your banker likes you and it is silly to maintain additional banking relationships for which you must pay. Pay the monthly bank charges willingly knowing that regardless of how fast the ax falls at bank A, you can literally transfer full financial control to Bank B or C in an afternoon.

Even if you must agree to do all your banking with a certain institution to get them to provide the debt financing you require, you can do this safely if you know you can quickly transfer all your funds to another bank if they threaten to call your loan or decide to require additional security interests or guarantees. When the bank realizes transfers have occurred and that you have choices, they will typically back off a little, and you can usually work something out.

The stupidest thing I ever did involving a bank was to set up a credit line. It was not a big line by banking standards, only $150,000 and since we used receivables as collateral, it was easy to obtain. I soon discovered however, just how dangerous a credit line could be. During an economic downturn, several of our clients filed bankruptcy and our lovely receivables that secured our line became "less than secure" in the bank's eyes. Our big bank's response was to call the line. In other words, they no longer wished to extend us credit and wanted us to either repay the line immediately or supply additional security. Fortunately, we had another bank that was more than pleased to be given the chance to take away business from the first bank. Because they were smaller, they saw this defection from the larger institution as a significant competitive accomplishment.

Why three banks and not two? Because at least fifty percent of the time, your second choice bank doesn't work either. You just need to have enough horses in your stable to always secure your financial escape. It's as simple as that.

I prefer small banks for the reasons stated above, but unfortunately, have found that smaller institutions have lending limits that make them impractical for some projects, particularly involving real estate. If this were not the case, I would do business with small banks exclusively. If your business is small enough so that lending limits do not enter into the equation, by all means, stick to smaller ones. Other than lending limits and the ability to handle foreign currency, I have yet to find a single benefit of selecting a large bank over a small one.

One final note to remember. Do not set up your personal bank accounts at any bank used by your business. In a banker's eyes, all your personal and business accounts make up just one big pile of money that can be tapped if anything goes wrong with the business. In banking, possession is not 9/10s of the law, it is the whole law. It they tap your personal accounts to satisfy a business debt, I guarantee you will never see a dime of your money again.

CHAPTER SEVENTY-FIVE

PAYCHECKS DO NOT FALL FROM HEAVEN

Running a business takes the heart of a gambler and the bank account of a casino. It should come as no surprise then, to find that entrepreneurs are often consumed with a single thought. "How do I find the cash to meet the payroll?"

Like most entrepreneurs, I assumed I would always pay myself in addition to my employees. This worked fine for a while because the startup money available to the business as seed capital was used to pay us all. As the business matured however, and the seed capital disappeared, things changed. Suddenly there was no guarantee there would be enough cash to meet the payroll. There was certainly no bank available to supply us with a financial safety net and we lacked the credit available to larger companies to get over the rough spots.

I had worked for other people for many years, prior to starting my own business. I was used to getting a paycheck. I had credit card bills to pay just like everyone else. So when the business had its first cash crisis and I realized that there was *no way* I would be able to pay myself, it was a rude awakening. How was I going to make my minimum payment to VISA? How was I going to write a check for groceries?

Had it not been for a decision made a number of years earlier, my entrepreneurial career would have been over. Many years before, my

254

husband and I had decided to live below our means. We did so originally, just for peace of mind, but once the decision was made to raise our level of risk by deciding to follow entrepreneurial pursuits, we found a much more compelling reason to stick to our decision.

Simply put, living below your means requires you to voluntarily limit your fixed obligations to a number well below your total take home pay. It means living in a house with a small mortgage, one that can easily be handled by a single income. Car payments need to be small or nonexistent and credit cards need to be kept available for both business and personal bailouts.

How do you tell if you are not living below your means? The symptoms are pretty obvious.

One day when I was dropping my daughter off at nursery school, I stopped at the front desk to pay her weekly tuition. Next to me stood a very handsome man whose 6'4" frame sported a hundred dollar shirt, gold cufflinks and three hundred dollar shoes. I had carefully parked my little Mercury Tracer station wagon next to his silver Mercedes in the parking lot.

He and I were waiting patiently for Wendy, the office manager to get off the phone. When she did so, he handed her two checks, each made out for $78.00. "This check is for last week," he said, holding out one of the checks. "This other check is for this week," he continued, "but please don't deposit it until the end of the month."

Manners eluded me. My mouth dropped open as I checked this guy out a second time. What was wrong with this picture? All of a sudden, all of my financial problems paled in comparison to the ones I imagined were standing next to me.

At least my Mercury Tracer was paid for. So were my shoes. I had $78.00 in the bank. Life was good!

My husband eventually joined the business, but during our start up years he remained employed by another company. Our thought at the time was to limit our standard of living to what one of us could earn in the outside world. If push came to shove, one of us in a traditional employment situation could carry the family while the other one did something silly like trying to start a business or worse, did something imprudent, like becoming seriously ill and unemployable.

Well, it has paid off. We have weathered innumerable financial storms with our little "live below your means" philosophy. It has allowed me to tell various bankers to take a leap, which I have found deeply satisfying and has given me the means to avoid layoffs when revenue in the business was temporarily depressed.

If you can readily remove yourself from the payroll from time to time, you will find it is often enough to allow you to meet the payroll expense of the remaining employees. The rewards associated with preventing layoffs are staggering. Just the savings in rehiring and retraining costs makes hanging in there through a tough month or two, well worth the pain.

There are just some ultimate truths in business that cannot be dodged. It is because of these truths that we, as entrepreneurs, do things like live below our means. It is the way we self-insure our businesses.

Chapter Seventy-Six

Three Clicks And You're Out

All across America, a new computer game is catching on. It's called *Three Clicks and You're Out.* It can be played on any computer and requires only two things, an Internet connection and a dumb boss.

It is easy to tell when the game is being played. Just walk into an employee's office without warning and see what happens. If he lunges for the mouse and CLICK, CLICK, CLICK, everything on his screen disappears, you can be sure he is hard at play doing one of the following:

- Looking for another job.

- Surfing the net.

- Writing personal e-mail.

- Working on his resume.

- Managing his stock portfolio.

- Participating in a chat room.

He wins of course, every time he succeeds in conducting play without detection. You win when you figure out how to stop him from playing in the first place.

Game time accounts for a significant loss of productivity in most companies and needs to be stopped. There are several steps you can take to stop this behavior.

First, treat all employees evenly. Publish a policy that prohibits the installation of personal software and restricts PC use to corporate tasks only. Next, get an enforcer to review, on a monthly basis, the software installed on all PCs in your company. Finally, if you have a firewall, install snooper software that will give you weekly reports on Internet access. Make sure your employees are all notified that this software is installed and that reports will be reviewed weekly.

If you find abuse, respond promptly and consistently. Do a formal warning and establish a probationary period. Dismiss any employee who repetitively violates the policy.

In one instance, I had an employee who persistently did the three click ritual when I entered his office. One night after he left, I entered his office and on a whim, decided to look in his trash basket. I found a scrap of paper with an e-mail address that sounded surprisingly X-rated. That was enough to motivate me to put a software package on his machine that tracked every keystroke made but was undetectable by the user.

After three days of monitoring I discovered he spent two to four hours every day e-mailing pornographic messages to dozens of people on the Internet. No wonder he couldn't make his sales quotas! The next day we presented him with a letter of resignation to sign and showed him a massive printout of his "X-rated" correspondence. He signed the letter, boxed up his things and walked out the door without saying a word.

Three click behavior is not always as onerous as this, but take it to heart. It's costing you money and needs to be stopped. You can get keystroke tracking software from a number of sources on the Internet for about $100.00. If you don't want to install sniffer software on your server, this is a great alternative and clearly *well* worth the price.

Chapter Seventy-Seven

Protect Your Employees—
Shut Down
The Abusive Customer

Why do some customers think they have a God given right to subject vendors to abuse? Their contracts certainly do not sanction bad behavior, yet it often continues for years, unabated. Like it or not, it is part of the entrepreneur's job to defend employees from tyrannical CEOs and irrational executives. Although this is certainly not a pleasant task, there is an up side. Defending the realm against unpleasant outsiders builds loyalty. Not the kind of loyalty that mumbles thank you, but the kind that causes employees to stick by you when the business is going through rough times.

I have seen abuse in its purest form on many occasions. The first time, the president of one of our biggest clients was the offender. He was a tall, good-looking, past-his-prime, ex-football player. To Barry, everything was a crisis. Everything needed to be done yesterday. And cussing at everyone and everything in his path was his tool of choice to get things done.

As one who remained uninitiated to the world of football, I was unaware that screaming profanity to get things done was standard operating procedure in the NFL. We were woefully unprepared for Barry. Our company didn't sport a bunch of people proficient in scratching and spitting, nor were athletic supporters in clear evidence around the office. We were under the mistaken impression that if you wanted to get someone to do something for you, the best way was to ask nicely. (Isn't that what Mom told us to do?)

Barry was immutable. We tried to calm him down. It didn't matter. Apparently he had a quota of swear words that he had to fulfill every day, for if, at the end of the day he was short, he blasted our receptionist, knowing that she had no one to transfer him to after hours. He didn't seem picky about the recipient; an ear was an ear.

I chalked up Barry's verbal assaults to too many days spent in the locker room with the boys. It brought our people to the breaking point on occasion, but everyone swallowed hard, and silently took his abuse. I really believed he was an isolated case, and after all, his company generated a lot of revenue for our firm. I just considered it a cost of doing business.

One day, while life continued unpleasantly with Barry, someone buzzed me on the intercom. "Sally's in tears," they said. "Andy from Unified Communications just swore at her on the phone. He just popped a gasket. You were on the other line and she didn't know what to do." Andy was the president of another of our clients. Andy was not the only one who popped.

All of a sudden my "isolated case" theory did not work. It wasn't just Barry. Others apparently thought they had the inalienable right to abuse. I felt like a sleeping lion that had just been rudely awakened. It was time to roar back. I picked up the phone to dial Andy's number.

After the five seconds I allotted him to say hello, I made sure he was unable to say another word for the next five minutes. "Andy," I said, "I need to make something perfectly clear to you. You have the right to good service. You have the right to receive a prompt response to your questions from my staff. You have a right to receive on-time and accurate billing. If any of these things fail to materialize, you have a right to voice your concerns. What you do not have a right to do is to abuse my people. I do not pay them to take verbal abuse. Their salaries are set to compensate them for the functions they perform, not to compensate them for being baited, humiliated, threatened or screamed at, and I will not allow you to subject them to this kind of treatment. If you have a problem and can't discuss it in a calm manner, you may ask to speak to me. It is my business and therefore I am "paid" to take whatever abuse you care to dish out, but I will not allow clients, or for that matter, anyone else, to abuse my people."

When I took a breath, Andy calmly replied, "You have to understand, I'm a New Yorker, and that's just how we are; we don't mean anything by it." "Well," I responded, "You reduced our secretary to tears. I have also learned that none of our customer service reps wish to speak to you because you are unwilling to carry on a civil conversation. Every conversation begins with threats, ultimatums and is peppered with foul language. At the rate you're going, the only one willing to talk to you is going to be me, and you will find my support skills sorely lacking. I am often out of the office and it may take a day or two for me to get back to you every time you call."

Much to my amazement, I got an, "Okay, I guess I'll have to remember that you guys are from Denver and not New York when I talk to you." That was it. He became reasonable on the phone (pleasant, for him was just too much of a stretch). The foul language all but stopped. The receptionist never got yelled at again. I couldn't believe it. Merely by calling his bluff, I had solved the problem. He was all show and no go and a true confrontation left him dead in his tracks.

Next I called Barry. I gave the same speech to him. He responded by canceling his contract. While we shed a few tears over the loss of his revenue, we did enjoy the office party that we held to commemorate the event.

I have *never* regretted confronting an abusive client. Employees are like family. They must be protected. You are the entrepreneurial parent and have an obligation to protect and provide for your employees. This extends to protecting them from situations they do not have the power or the authority to control. Being protected is one of their benefits, like healthcare. If you fail to supply your end of the bargain, they have every right to leave you for breach of the contract you implied when you hired them.

I find it quite interesting that the individuals dishing out the abuse have been, without exception, either presidents or vice presidents of their organizations. By contrast, their employees have consistently displayed pleasant and problem-solving attitudes even when their companies were not the cause of the problem. What then, caused these particular individuals to toss out all known rules of etiquette and lace into people as a God given right?

The answer is simple. These people think they are better, bigger and badder than anyone else in the neighborhood. They act like bullies because they think their rank will allow them to get away with acting like brats. They are no different than children, who unless reprimanded, beat up everyone in sight, that is, until a bully bigger than themselves comes to town.

Let me introduce you to a bigger bully. It is the one you see when you look in the mirror. Accept the challenge and step up to protect the people who work for you. You may lose some business from time to time, but you will build bonds within your company that are surprisingly strong. It will make you feel good about yourself. It will make your employees feel good about you.

Chapter Seventy-Eight

Take The Good Stuff Home

Do you think the only snoops in your life are your kids scouting the house for Christmas presents? Wrong. Employees often hone snooping to a fine art as well. Far from amusing, this is a dangerous activity and needs to be taken seriously by every entrepreneur.

Information gained through snooping fuels competitive fires between employees, reduces productivity by changing people's focus to things that don't concern them, and frequently causes employees to worry about things that are beyond their control.

People have varied snooping styles. There are those who are adept at reading upside down. Others make a habit of "accidentally" observing what is on your desktop every time they deliver papers to your office. Hi-tech snoops consider it a measure of their technical prowess to find ways to break into the corporate payroll system or scan the network for personnel reviews. Some people just like to go through your desk when you're not there just to see if they can find anything interesting.

Inadvertent snooping can also be a problem. When you discuss sensitive topics with others, conversations can often be heard plainly in the next office, and it seldom takes long for astute employees to take advantage of this opportunity.

I cannot over-emphasize the damage that can be done by snooping. A careless bookkeeper once left payroll records unattended while she went to lunch. By the time she returned, the entire company was aware of what everyone else made. Everyone was angry. Everyone felt cheated, underpaid, under appreciated, and wanted immediate changes in their own compensation. It was a nightmare that lasted for more than a year.

My solution to this has been to implement the anti-snoop checklist. While it certainly doesn't prevent all snooping, it does cut down on snooping opportunities and definitely helps reduce office politics.

THE ANTI-SNOOP CHECKLIST

1. Never store sensitive documents in your office. Store them in your briefcase until you can take them home and then leave them there.

2. Make sure those delivering papers to other offices place them face down in the recipient's inbox.

3. Make sure all storage areas in the accounting department lock.

4. Place all accounting personnel in real offices with doors that close.

5. Store computerized personnel information on removable storage media and lock these disks up.

6. Take old records off site, preferably to your basement at home. A room containing archived files is an often overlooked source for employees who really want to dig for information because they can conduct a thorough search for something without fear of being interrupted.

7. Do not make your accounting system part of the corporate computer network. Make it separate and assign someone in the accounting department to do any required system administration functions.

8. Test how soundproof your offices and meeting rooms are. We found that covering gaps in wall dividers with plastic strips helped soundproof many problem offices.

9. Make sure all employees use a screen-saver password on their computers, so current work remains secure during temporary absences.

10. Make security a topic of discussion in your company. Let people know that you expect them to respect the privacy of other people's work and that they themselves are expected to follow good security practices.

Keeping snooping to a minimum keeps everyone focused on his own business, not on everyone else's. It's just one more way to make sure you maintain a productive organization with a good attitude.

OPINIONS THAT COUNT

CHAPTER SEVENTY-NINE

IT's NOT WRONG
UNTIL IT's OUT THE DOOR

If a tree falls in the forest and no one hears it, does it make any sound? Only if the sound reaches a client's ear. Everything else is virtual reality. No matter how big a mistake is, it doesn't matter if it never makes it out the door.

One day the phone rang. It was Bob, the president of one of our client companies. I always enjoyed sparring with Bob, who relished discovering every little anomaly in our operation. We good-naturedly discussed how to eke every last dollar out of his billing each month.

"I just talked to someone who called me as a reference for you guys," he said. "After I gave him my spiel, he shut me down with a question. He asked me something nobody ever asked before, so I had to think about it. When I finally came up with something, I thought it was so profound, I had to call you up to tell you about it."

I sat down with a thud, feeling depressed. "Okay, here it comes," I thought. "I bet Bob has loaded both barrels." He continued. "He asked me, 'What makes these guys different?' You know I'm an attorney. I *always* have something to whip right back. I think I was actually silent for over a minute." I knew Bob pretty well. I was as amazed by this as he was. A silent attorney; now there's a contradiction in terms. I knew we were both smiling at the thought. I took a deep breath. "Okay Bob, the suspense is killing me. What did you come up with?" "You care," he said.

269

That certainly wasn't an answer in keeping with Bob's flamboyant personality; in fact, it was downright boring. "That's it?" I asked. "Yeah, that's it." He sounded so proud. I felt sorry for him. Perhaps he'd had a rough day. I didn't say anything. Bob didn't seem to notice and kept going. "You care if there is a smudge on my bills. You call me if a dozen calls wind up in an error file and can't be billed. You worry if the payments I entered in the system seem lower than last month. These days, nobody cares. You care like the money I'm going to collect is your own." I didn't have the heart to tell Bob that my retentive personality and his retentive personality were key components in the equation. "Gee Bob," I said. "Thanks for caring enough to tell me all about this." I dug deep to conjure up a tone of heartfelt sincerity. Certainly it was a nice comment but not exactly earth shattering.

Eventually I decided Bob's comment *was* earth shattering. He had made an astute observation and identified our key to success. Bob was excited because we *always* took the trouble to check. We didn't make any fewer mistakes than anyone else, we were just more concerned about catching them and this simple attribute separated us from our competition.

I can't think of any business more prone to problems and errors than complex data processing. You constantly chase your tail, as modifications reveal new opportunities to mess up something that historically worked like a charm. The trick is to put into place checks and balances that will insure that problems can consistently be detected before resulting mistakes make it out the door.

As a manager, the secret is to accept the failings of human beings and focus on catching, not preventing, every conceivable mistake. People are certainly not perfect, but with good quality control procedures in place, they don't have to be.

Don't try to create perfect employees. Try to create perfect controls. The goal is certainly more achievable, and every now and then a grateful customer will notice that you seem to "care" just a little more than your competition.

Chapter Eighty

Even Your Receptionist Doesn't Know For Sure

Although it is human nature to explore areas of common interest by offering information about yourself, resist the temptation when it comes to your staff. Keeping some distance between yourself and your employees is the best way to insure that your staff stays focused on your business and not on you.

Natural curiosity will always cause those who work for you to speculate about the less publicized aspects of your life. Worse yet, employees will freely apply their own subjective tests to decide whether you work hard enough, are fair enough, spend enough time at the office, drive a reasonable car or take too much money out of the business. These speculative activities will occur despite your efforts to quell them, so it is important to learn how to build safe relationships without adding fuel to speculative fires.

Relationships are safe when the information given to the other party does not expose emotional weakness, or reveal information or opinions that should not be disclosed to others. The trick is to learn how to stay within this definition when sharing information with employees. In my case, I learned this lesson the hard way. I learned it on the road.

My first job was as an auditor for the State of Ohio. I was on the road five days a week driving my state supplied Plymouth Valiant from company to company conducting audits. I was on a rotating auditing team of six people. The pool of auditors from which groups were assigned consisted of about twenty-five men, all of whom were over thirty. This meant that I was always with five older guys who had spent years on the road together. Most of you can probably imagine what transpired, but for those who can't, let me share.

The object of the game was to make me feel I was the odd man (or woman) out. The "boys" would have been much happier if I had been rolled over by my Plymouth. They liked their good ol' boy way of life and resented my forced addition to their group. They made cracks about how much luggage women bring. They regaled me with an endless stream of dirty jokes. They constantly winked and chuckled to each other. The older ones tried to treat me like a little kid who knew nothing. I was twenty-five years old and miserable.

One evening in my motel room I made a decision. I would no longer give them the fuel they needed to make me miserable. I would not react to their remarks. I would ignore their dirty jokes. I suddenly realized that I did not need to share anything with them. They were not part of my personal support group. They were coworkers. Their opinion of me was irrelevant. I only had to please my boss.

I stopped sharing. I limited conversations to business and shared only information that related to what we were doing. I kept conversations regarding my personal life to a minimum. Lo and behold, things started to improve. I became braver. I started to tell dirty jokes in response to their jokes. I made a point of never blushing. I disregarded any slights made and watched their dejected faces out of the corner of my eye. I soon prevailed. They gave up.

Before long, they accepted me as a coworker, an almost gender neutral addition to the work group. Over the years, I actually developed a pleasant relationship with several of the men but on my terms. The days of testing were over.

When I began my own company, it was in many ways reminiscent of my early days as an auditor. I was still tested and talked about behind my back, just for different reasons. I was not part of the group, not because of my sex but because of my status in the organization. I soon realized that control of the situation could be obtained the same way.

Once again, I restricted what I told people about my personal life. I did not explain my whereabouts even to the receptionist. I only told her I would be out of the office for a specified period of time. I ignored the hastily whispered remarks in the halls and the amused haughty glances that told me I was, at that moment, the subject of conversation. I made it clear I just didn't care.

Once again, things improved. Business as usual prevailed. I eventually found that I could share personal things with employees, but that these things needed to be concrete events, not my opinions or feelings about things. Emotional outpourings are the things that undermine your authority and fuel the gossip mills.

Give careful thought to what you reveal about your personal life to others. At a minimum they will formulate opinions about your character. More likely, they will form opinions that will result in a lack of respect for you that will ultimately undermine your authority.

Do not look to your employees for emotional support. Get support from outside the organization and keep those working for you outside your circle of confidants. Your business should support you financially, not emotionally.

CHAPTER EIGHTY-ONE

TYPOS, A DEADLY DISEASE

Do you remember diagramming sentences in your youth? You do? Then you are probably old enough to know the difference between a pronoun and a participle. Unfortunately, many younger members of today's work force know little about the parts of speech. Particularly during the seventies and eighties, educators focused on "relating" to children instead of teaching them. (After all, children might not like school if we make it too hard.) We are now reaping the dubious benefits of tree-hugger education.

New hires cannot spell. They screw up the tenses in their sentences. They have no clue why anyone would ever use a semicolon. "Oh," everyone says, "That's not a problem. We have spell check and grammar check now." Au contraire. Spell check fails to find the classic form/from typo. Grammar check is useless. Last time I used it, it underlined in blue virtually everything I wrote. It apparently wasn't programmed for some of the legitimate constructs I cared to use. I threatened to retire my PC to the dumpster via my second story window.

Why am I obsessed with typos? Because the most important messages sent in business are the subliminal ones. "If you don't care enough to proof your e-mail to me, why would you care that the work you perform for me is accurate?" the client wonders. Even more important, it plants dangerous seeds of doubt. "If they have no quality control on the correspondence they send, why should I assume there is any quality control imposed on the products they produce for me?" Good question.

I obsess about quality. I always require client-addressed e-mail to be bcc'd (blind carbon copied) to me so I can monitor the quality of the correspondence our company sends out.

Grammatical accuracy seems like such a little thing, but I am pulled up short each time I receive an e-mail full of typos and grammatical errors. I stop reading the e-mail for content and start tearing it apart to surmise how educated the author is and more importantly, how much the author cares about my opinion. Usually I conclude, not much.

People's grammar and spelling can be improved, but it is a long and arduous road to travel. I often take my famous green pen and laboriously correct someone's e-mail, writing grammatical rules in the margin and circling the spelling errors. Actually, employees working for me could easily rate my opinion of their value to the company using this system. Because it takes tremendous time to edit an e-mail when the objective is to educate the author, anyone who is subjected to this pain can count themselves among the most valued in the company. If I don't think they will stick, I never go to the trouble.

I want our company to stand out among the crowd. I want our clients to focus on the content of the e-mails they receive from us, not on the typos. I want the subliminal message to be, "Boy, those guys always seem to have their act together. Not even the smallest detail escapes them."

Identify the individuals in your company who can write effectively and accurately. Set them up in the "review chain" and make sure that someone with writing expertise has an opportunity to review the e-mails of those less fortunate employees who cannot string a decent sentence together. Do it *before* e-mails are sent.

Certainly spell check is not perfect, but it is far better than the unbridled creativity of employees. Require spell check to be turned on and confirm the fact periodically. Grammar check is more trouble than it's worth. By using the review chain, the need for grammar check is certainly lessened and the human touch it provides does educationally what no software program could ever do.

Be proactive about training the educationally less fortunate to write so that over time, the time (and therefore the cost) of authoring and correcting e-mail correspondence will drop. Investing in an employee's skill as a writer will produce a good return on investment. Accuracy builds customer confidence and confidence builds a solid foundation for customer relationships.

A typo may seem like a little thing, but as Benjamin Franklin said, "If you will merely watch the pennies, you will find the dollars will take care of themselves." You betcha, Ben.

Chapter Eighty-Two

On The Fifth Ring, Dive For The Phone

Please listen carefully to the following seven choices and select the option that best meets your needs. Your call may be monitored or recorded to assure quality or for training purposes. Did you know we now have an Internet address to quickly answer your questions? Just type www.ourtimeismoreimportantthanyours.com and aimlessly follow menu selections and hot links until you are frustrated enough to log off and call us to complain.

To talk to a sales representative, press one. (Sales is always first. After all, shouldn't we solicit new business before we take care of existing customers?) For your account balance or other trivial information that you don't really care about, press two. To check on your order to find out why it never shipped or has been lost, press three. To compliment us on the wonderful job we are doing, press four. To insure that you will never be able to leave this voice mail system during your natural lifetime, press five. To yell at the president who will not answer, nor will she listen to any voice mail message you decide to leave, press six. To talk to a customer service representative, please stay on the line so we may keep you on hold listening to dentist office music which we will interrupt periodically with "All representatives are busy at this time, please stay on the line in case we ever decide to take your call."

You know you are done of course, when you receive, "If you would like to make a call, please hang up and try your call again."

If I call again and dial the same stupid number I will go through the same stupid stuff and get the same stupid recording! That's almost as dumb as the notice on the back of airplane seats, PLEASE FASTEN SEAT BELT WHILE SEATED. No, I think I would rather try to do it standing up while I contemplate why Hawaii has interstate highways.

Has the definition of customer service been expunged from everyone's dictionary? I want to talk to a real person! I want them to listen to me and supply a coherent, responsive answer. What a concept!

Until three years ago, our company didn't have voice mail. Torn between the convenience of voice mail for the supplier and the irritation it creates for the user, we sought some sort of middle ground. Finally, we decided that all people calling our company would be greeted by a warm human being. Voice mail would be relegated solely to taking messages after hours or recording messages for unavailable employees *after* the caller had been asked if they wished to leave a voice mail message.

I still detest voice mail, but its judicious use does allow our staff to get a jump on obtaining responses to client inquiries so that they frequently have the answer to a voice mail question when the call is returned.

This mode of operation leads to another problem, however. It is the unanswered phone. A phone that rings more than five times tells our clients one of the following things.

1. **We are too busy to answer our phone properly.** "Maybe," thinks the caller, "they are too busy to handle *me* properly."

2. **We don't care that a caller has to wait for an interminable number of rings before his call is answered.** We are sending a clear message to the caller that we don't think answering his call is a business priority.

3. **We feel our time is more important than our client's time.** This is the message all voice mail systems send and is the message we are trying to avoid in the first place.

4. **We are not really concerned with the impression we are giving a client who calls in**. "After all," thinks the caller, "I am not a sales prospect any more, just an existing customer who will be made to wait until calls from sales prospects are handled."

At our company we solve this by diving for the phone on the fifth ring. Not everyone dives in the same order, however. On the first or second ring, everyone assumes the receptionist will answer. On the third ring, the "inner circle" is expected to dive for the phone. This includes female customer service representatives and female accounting staff members. On the fourth ring, all female employees should be diving. On the fifth ring, *everyone* should dive.

Why do women dive for the phone before men? Because we live in a stereotypical world where the impression we give by a man answering the phone is that (a) we are a small company, (b) we are understaffed, or (c) the company "marches to a different drum." I do not want any of these impressions left with our callers.

My office is located where I am out of earshot of ringing outside lines. For this reason, I had the phone system programmed to make my phone ring quietly to allow me to be in the pool of outside phone line answerers. This sends a message to both employees and customers. NO ONE is immune from answering the phone. We are all customer service representatives, no matter what our job title is.

When, on occasion, I do answer an outside line and the client calling recognizes my voice, they always get a kick out of it and come up with some sort of quip in response. Quip aside however, it is obvious from their tone that the message "we really care about giving quality support to our customers," has been delivered with a vengeance. I have never found a customer who didn't like discovering that his customer service representative was also the president.

Make a point to pay attention to the subliminal messages your company may be sending. These are frequently far more important than overt messages, yet they seldom get the attention they deserve. Diving for the phone is one of these. It is a powerful way to separate yourself from the masses and it's fun to be known as a company that provides service the good old fashioned way, just because it's the way it ought to be done.

CHAPTER EIGHTY-THREE

BASHING LEADS TO BANKRUPTCY

Are you a little cynical? Does every glass appear half empty to you? Do you have a smart remark for every occasion? I certainly do. My somewhat askance view of life frequently causes my husband to say, "Don't hold back, tell me what you really think," as I am ripping off one of my brutally honest, if less than tactful, observations.

Despite the pleasure I take from lambasting thoughtless drivers and obnoxious TV personalities, I have to admit that my caustic comments have a down side. They often cause trouble when they invade conversations about business.

One of the things I find hardest about running a business is being my own disciplinarian. I know what I *should* do; I just can't seem to do it. The lure of doing what I want to do instead of what I should do is often just too great. When I realized I would have to stop verbally bashing clients in order to encourage employees to appreciate and respect our clients, I was horrified to find I lacked the willpower to do so.

Typically meetings started off in a civil enough manner, but often, as a meeting progressed, some situation would arise that just begged for me to leap in with some caustic comment.

Usually things started nicely enough. "Why can't we proceed with billing for Friendly Phones, Inc?" I would ask. "Because they hired somebody new and forgot to train them on our system," someone would answer. "Don't worry about it," I would chime in. "Their data entry person used to work for McDonald's, and they're having trouble typing because the pictures are missing; they can't find the hamburger key. Who wants to be a good sport, and offer to train them?" Usually everyone giggled, either because they really thought it was funny or because to do so was part of the corporate brownie code.

Once the ball was rolling, others felt free to jump in. References to Big Macs and french fries or other equally unflattering analogies proliferated and many times, became permanently associated with the client victim. At first, this behavior appeared harmless. But as with most insidious problems, its roots ran deep before the damage became apparent. Humor was soon displaced by a lack of respect. Lack of respect led to unresponsiveness. Unresponsiveness contributed to poor service. Poor service resulted in client attrition.

What started as a harmless comment made solely for my own amusement became a deadly corporate disease that I was unable to cure. What's more, I had great difficulty in repressing my stream-of-consciousness mouth, *even knowing the consequences of my comments!*

What I ultimately realized was that through my flippant comments, I released my frustrations with clients toward whom I felt hostile and wished to retaliate, despite business etiquette to the contrary. How ironic that the method I selected to release my frustrations got rid of the source of those frustrations as well. The result might be good for my mental health, but it was definitely bad for the bottom line. What I needed was a more acceptable and financially viable emotional outlet if the business was going to survive.

Did I cure myself of making costly snide comments? No. I learned to counterbalance instead. Each time a comment did slip out, I attempted to disarm it by following it with a heartfelt message of appreciation, thanking the client I just lambasted for paying our light bill and covering our salaries. I did not try to pretend that they were easy to get along with or that I loved them. I merely mentioned that they had their good points and that tolerance of their bad points was a business necessity. "We provide service, therefore we are," became a credo of sorts that said, this is our lot in life. We accept its challenges, even on our client's "bad days."

This offsetting tune, sung after each misstep, did a lot to get respect back into our client vocabulary. In a way, it put our business and our client businesses on the same level. None of us were perfect, and on our bad days we could still take that pot shot or two. Yet, cooler heads prevailed after each bashing episode, and the result was that we all returned to our duties with an appreciation for the entrepreneurial pressures and concerns we shared with our clients.

Do I wish I could cure myself of snide comments altogether? Maybe, on some days. On others, I'm glad to be reminded that the personnel problems we moan about as owners are often staring at us in the mirror, reflected in our very human faces.

CHAPTER EIGHTY-FOUR

MANAGEMENT BY LEVEL OF RISK

Bob and Larry were two type A, overachiever managers. Each had a significant fiefdom as Bob managed Operations and Larry was in charge of Program Development. During virtually every staff meeting, these two guys locked horns and flexed their managerial muscles, while the group waited to see who would prevail through superior intimidation skills. Week after week the animosity continued until confrontation between these two became a weekly ritual.

One day a particularly important decision was on the table. It involved determining which group was to be responsible for managing the company's Local Area Network (LAN). The system was used for corporate communications and by programmers doing development. Both Bob and Larry wanted to control the network and both clearly thought the decision should be theirs. As voices became louder and each began slinging accusations, I lost what little patience I had left. I decided to shut down both of them.

"Constant conflict between the two of you does nothing but raise our corporate blood pressure and irritate me! It's time to alleviate the stress for everyone involved. Beginning today we are going to adopt a new policy. We will now make all decisions at this company based solely on level of risk." The room went silent as I took the wind out of each combatant's sail. In fact, a breeze did not stir over our corporate ocean for several minutes. "Let me tell you how this is going to work," I began.

"Let's look at the decision that's on the table. Bob and Larry have very different opinions on the subject. So, assuming neither Bob nor Larry can convince the other that their opinion is correct, someone is going to win and someone is going to lose." The rolling of eyes around the room told me the group had decided my I.Q. could certainly be measured in single digits. Undaunted, I continued. "We will begin by deciding, ahead of time, who the prevailing party will be in every argument. We will do this by evaluating each party's level of risk."

"Bob, assigning corporate LAN support to Operations makes sense because your group currently maintains the other computer systems in the company and all of these systems are interconnected with the LAN."

"Larry, no one disputes that if the system goes down, your group is severely impacted. Program Development however, has no knowledge of the other systems interconnected with the LAN and your staff could easily disrupt these systems while performing LAN maintenance."

"This decision is not very difficult. The risk of having interconnected production systems go down when they are unwittingly affected by LAN maintenance is far greater than the risk that the development team will be temporarily unable to do their work due to a maintenance outage. This one is a no brainer. Bob, as head of Operations, your level of risk is definitely higher. If the two of you can't work out a mutually acceptable solution, Bob, you get to win."

The group woke up at this point, as the "teeth" of the philosophy had now been exposed. "Let me add the last piece of the puzzle," I said. "If it is not obvious to those in conflict who possesses the interest that is most at risk, a third, uninterested party will make that determination. In this company, that person will be me.

From that day on, meetings took on a whole new tone. The arguments all but ceased because those in attendance could readily determine the department with the greatest level of risk, and they knew I would enforce the policy if they failed to make a determination on their own.

Life is much more peaceful now, and to make sure the peace continues, I deliver the following speech to everyone I hire.

"There is no difference between you and me in this company unless we can't come to an agreement on something. If we disagree, and you can't convince me that your position has more merit than mine, I get to win. The reason I get to win is because my level of risk within the company is higher. Because I have to ultimately worry about everything in the business, including its solvency and its long term viability, my level of risk is the highest in the organization."

"This same rule applies throughout the company. If an employee and his manager fail to come to an agreement, then the manager gets to win. If two peers within the company fail to agree, we apply a test to see who has the higher level of risk. In every decision, there is always someone who is more severely affected by the outcome than anyone else. In twenty-five years of using this method, I have never seen a tie. Someone's level of risk is *always* higher."

After making this speech, I have never had a new hire question why we use this method. It appears the inherent logic of this approach is readily apparent.

Decision-making by level of risk has many subtle benefits. It spares the egos of individuals who disagree by removing personalities from the decision-making process. It stops political behavior because it is not possible to affect decisions by coercion or ego stroking. Most important, it effectively cultivates mutual respect between adversarial departments because the process of analyzing risks reveals departmental burdens and responsibilities which would normally not be visible to other groups.

Decision-making by level of risk is the most important principal driving my business. I simply cannot over emphasize its importance. If you have doubts, try it. You have nothing to lose but wasted time and aggravation.

Chapter Eighty-Five

Office Beauty Matters

Many years ago, I took over a company that was on the brink of failure. The owners and investors had asked me to take over and they all assumed I would relocate to the choice office vacated by my predecessor. Wrong. I don't like big offices. I don't like windows. I like cozy little offices that I can nest in and limit distractions to a bare minimum. Everyone thought I was crazy when I selected a small interior office without windows. Que Sera.

Unlike myself, most employees seem to spend endless hours fretting over environmental issues that I consider trivial. I have witnessed two employees duke it out over a corner office with a view. I have seen people cease speaking because their desk overhangs were different. I have listened to endless complaints because someone else had a bigger bookcase. I have seen pouting that would do justice to a two-year-old because somebody's chair would not tilt like their neighbor's. It never ends.

Now I am relatively impervious to environmental factors. As long as it's quiet, I'm happy. Because of my own indifferences, I have always given lip service to the demands/whining of employees who were not happy with their little worlds. I always felt that if someone was that unhappy, they could vote with their feet.

286

Now let's talk about important things. What's really important in an office is peace and quiet. If I hear someone whistling, I can think of several commandments I would cheerfully violate to *stop that whistling!* But whistling is serious. We all understand that off-key whistling is more irritating than fingernails on a chalk board ... don't we?

Could there be a parallel between my need for peace and quiet and somebody's need to view something besides the parking lot? Of course not. What I consider important, is important. What you consider important is trivial if it doesn't bother me. Let's see. I think I have just stated, dare I say it, the legendary SEC (Selfish Entrepreneur's Credo).

I am ashamed to admit how long it took me to realize that what is important to someone else is still important even if it is not important to me and for that very reason, my antennae should go up each time someone voices a heartfelt concern.

When I dismiss a request as silly, I have failed to show respect for the person making the request. I have sent her the signal that her worth to the company is not adequate to make me take her request seriously.

Well, better late than never. I still think a lot of the concerns I hear are stupid, but then lots of people thought I was a moron for refusing an eight-foot desk in a fifteen by twenty foot office with a panoramic view of the city in two directions.

Tell your employees you value them with actions as well as words. If they want a different desk chair, get them one. If they need an additional file cabinet, hand them the office supply catalog and give them a "not to exceed" amount they can spend. Treat them like adults and treat them with respect.

The adage, "We reap what we sow," remains as true today as it was 2,000 years ago. I can't think of any better seeds to sow in a business than those from which respect will grow. It is relationships built upon respect that form the root structure supporting every successful business.

A FINAL WORD

CHAPTER EIGHTY-SIX

GIVING CREDIT WHERE CREDIT IS DUE

Even the chapters that appear to have nothing to do with my father contain his powerful life philosophy. Live honestly. Treat others with respect. Use your brain. Enjoy the simple pleasures of life. Take pride in what you do. Make a difference. Add a little humor along the way. The way he looked at life is the real gift he gave to me.

One day, as I was going through some files, I came across the pages that follow, which he had written thirty-five years before. First I smiled. Then I laughed out loud. The essence of the book I had just written was staring back at me. My father had written ten "advisories," each of which he had sent as a daily memo to one of his reportees. They were written in my father's memorable, if less than subtle style, to drive home one of his favorite points, the importance of effective communication.

I could shut my eyes and hear his voice. "Your book's not bad, just too long. Too bad you didn't follow Strunk!"

Well there's always room for improvement. Long or not, I think Dad would think it worthy of a chuckle and a smile to see his own philosophy put to work.

I guess the apple never falls far from the tree.

April 1, 1969

To: D. L. Fitz   From: R. N. Haigh

ADVISORY BULLETIN #1 (of 10)

Gen. Anthony Clement McAuliffe, U.S. Army
December 23, 1944

"NUTS"

Care and try to improve on this?

Note: The German's demand that allied troops surrender during World
War II was met with General McAuliffe's emphatic refusal "Nuts!" that
led to the eventual defeat of the German advance during the Battle of the
Bulge.

April 2, 1969

To: D. L. Fitz   From: R. N. Haigh

ADVISORY BULLETIN #2 (of 10)

The Gettysburg Address is less than 300 words.

April 3, 1969

To: D. L. Fitz   From: R. N. Haigh

ADVISORY BULLETIN #3 (of 10)

Norman Bel Geddes, Industrial Designer, was hired by the New York Central Railroad to redesign their locomotives. To get a feel for the problem he rode from New York to Buffalo in the cab of an engine. He was met by a group of New York Central executives who wanted to know immediately if he had any suggestions. He said yes, "Put a toilet in the engine cab."

In seven words he:

  (a)   stated the engineering problem.

  (b)   stated the solution to it.

  (c)   expressed a social opinion.

  (d)   indicated his opinion of the management capabilities of the New York Central executives.

Not bad for seven words!

April 4, 1969

To: D. L. Fitz   From: R. N. Haigh

ADVISORY BULLETIN #4 (of 10)

Sighted sub, sank same.

Donald Francis Mason

April 7, 1969

To: D. L. Fitz   From: R. N. Haigh

ADVISORY BULLETIN #5 (of 10)

My daughter Marsha was born April 28, 1955.
In the preceding November I wrote my mother
a letter. At this time my brother was not
married. A duplicate of the letter is attached.

Do you think you can improve on this as a
brief message?

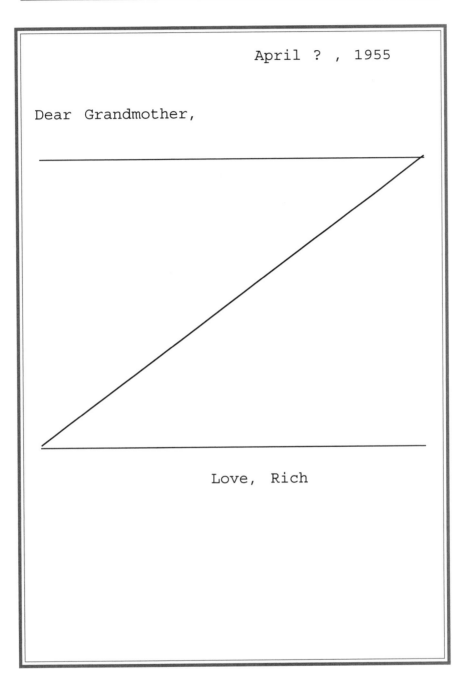

April ? , 1955

Dear Grandmother,

Love, Rich

April 8, 1969

To: D. L. Fitz   From: R. N. Haigh

ADVISORY BULLETIN #6 (of 10)

Some smart man recommends that one should "proposition every girl you meet. If you get a two percent return on your investment, you're going like hell." This is pretty good advice except it's incomplete. I recommend you make it a short proposition to keep your volume up. After all, two percent of one girl is a very unhandy amount.

MORAL: Instructions can be too brief.

April 9, 1969

To: D. L. Fitz   From: R. N. Haigh

ADVISORY BULLETIN #7 (of 10)

Once upon a time a Harvard Business School
Graduate, contemplating motivational theory
while walking beside the sea, found a Chivas
Regal bottle. Chivas being a BBD&O* account
and therefore "in", he opened the bottle to
find he had released a genie who immediately offered to grant a wish as a reward
for his freedom.

The HBSG promptly requested that he never
grow any older (he currently having the
world by the tail) as his wish. The genie
asked him if he was absolutely certain that
this was exactly what he wanted as his reward, and being assured that it was, granted
the wish.

The HBSG dropped dead on the spot.

MORAL: "Communication skills" is a tricky
subject.

*Batton, Barton, Durstin & Osborne

April 10, 1969

To: D. L. Fitz   From: R. N. Haigh

ADVISORY BULLETIN #8 (of 10)

A rose is a rose is a rose is a rose.

Gertrude Stein

It may be poetry, but what is the message?

April 11, 1969

To: D. L. Fitz   From: R. N. Haigh

ADVISORY BULLETIN #9 (of 10)

If we go on explaining, we shall cease to
understand one another.

Talleyrand

April 14, 1969

To: D. L. Fitz   From: R. N. Haigh

ADVISORY BULLETIN #10 (of 10)

He draweth out the thread of his verbosity
finer than the staple of his argument.

Shakespeare — Love's
Labours Lost IV ii 25

THANKS, DAD

Index To Chapters

DATE DUE